*Journey*
*Blissful Life*

Beloved family and friends,

Bliss is a kiss to the soul. And the journey can be oh so sweet.

Imagine a life of divinity, rather than one hell-bent on destroying life and liberties.

Imagine a life of spirit and simplicity, rather than of gutlessness and duplicity.

Imagine a life that is not in havoc, but in harmony with the universe.

Imagine a global call for the uplifting of the soul, not through the sometimes narrowed eyes of religion, but from the enlightened eye of humanity.

Imagine a life overflowing with joy, grace, tenderness, compassion, and abundance.

Imagine where the world would be if it could hear women sing.

*Journey to a Blissful Life* is our hymn.

With gratitude,
Maria

# Journey to a Blissful Life

## Maria D. Dowd

BET Publications, LLC
http://www.bet.com

NEW SPIRIT BOOKS are published by

BET Publications, LLC
c/o BET BOOKS
One BET Plaza
1900 W Place NE
Washington, DC 20018-1211

Copyright © 2005 by Maria Denise Dowd

All rights reserved. No part of this book may be reproduced, stored in a retrieval system, or transmitted in any form or by any means without the prior written consent of the Publisher.

If you purchased this book without a cover, you should be aware that this book is stolen property. It was reported as "unsold and destroyed" to the Publisher and neither the Author nor the Publisher has received any payment for this "stripped book."

All Kensington Titles, Imprints, and Distributed Lines are available at special quantity discounts for bulk purchases for sales promotions, premiums, fund-raising, and educational or institutional use. Special book excerpts or customized printings can also be created to fit specific needs. For details, write or phone the office of the Kensington Special Sales Manager: Attn. Special Sales Department, Kensington Publishing Corp., 850 Third Avenue, New York, NY 10022, Phone: 1-800-221-2647.

BET Books is a trademark of Black Entertainment Television, Inc. NEW SPIRIT and the NEW SPIRIT logo are trademarks of BET Books and the BET BOOKS logo is a registered trademark.

Library of Congress Card Catalogue Number: 2004110648
ISBN: 1-58314-497-8

First Printing: June 2005
10  9  8  7  6  5  4  3  2  1

Printed in the United States of America

# *ACKNOWLEDGMENTS*

This book is dedicated to my African American Women on Tour (AAWOT) sisterfriends, to Warm Spirit's AAWOT Angels, and to my sister contributors whose voices chime intently with clarity and truth. On our individual and collective journeys toward greater peace, wellness, bliss, and abundance, all of you have been and continue to be integral parts of the Flow. I trust that you've gained as much from my work on this planet as I have from all of you. Our arms reach around the globe a thousand times, and our hands and hearts are bound eternally by hope, passion, and faith. I thank God daily for having afforded me the gift of African American Women on Tour that serves as the universal connective tissue.

I also extend the wholeness of my heart to Rafiki Cai, a prophet in his own right, who has taught me a lesson or two about moon men and their sun-fired women. Through the helping hand of God, my insights are stretched beyond the realm. Rafiki, you're a divine creative force that spans beyond the cosmos. Know it, and show it, Dear Spirit.

And a special thanks to Linda Gill for paving the way, to Jaynelle St. Jean for clearing away the debris, and to my family and friends who bring so much light into my life with love, laughter, and encouragement.

# CONTENTS

## JOURNEY TO FAITH AND SPIRITUALITY

| | |
|---|---|
| **Perfectly Divine Mates** by Kamilah Hasan | 3 |
| **Getting There** by Maria Denise Dowd | 7 |
| **Tête-à-tête** by Rafiki Cai | 13 |
| **Retreat, Reflect, and Advance** by Caroline Shola Arewa | 21 |
| **Just for Today** by Reverend Victoria Lee-Owens | 27 |
| **Journey to Healing** by Carolyn Ross | 28 |
| **The Other Side of the Canyon** by Chanequa Walker-Barnes | 39 |
| **And I Cried** by Kallene Rutherford | 45 |
| **Introduction: Waiting for a Miracle** by Beverley East | 47 |
| **Journey to Love: The Circle of Love** by Ayesha Grice | 50 |
| **Love Is** by Erica Sheppard | 53 |
| **A Sister-Kinda Love** by Beverley East | 56 |
| **A True Love Story** by Monique Brown McKenzie | 61 |
| **O My Divine** by Emily Diane Gunter | 72 |

## JOURNEY TO PEACE AND SERENITY

| | |
|---|---|
| **Miss Grace Is in the House** by Maria Denise Dowd | 75 |
| **Unearthed** by Gequeta Valentine | 79 |
| **Rearview Mirror** by Maria Denise Dowd | 84 |

| | |
|---|---|
| **No More** by Shellie Warren | 88 |
| **The Peace Process** by Debrena Jackson Gandy | 94 |
| **A Matter of Taste** by Mary Elizabeth Paschall | 99 |
| **Love Thy Neighbor** by Nicole Gailliard | 100 |
| **Love Affair** by Kimberly T. Matthews | 104 |
| **Maturity** by Reverend Victoria Lee-Owens | 107 |
| **Our Quest for Peace** by Maria Denise Dowd and Jewel Diamond Taylor | 111 |
| **Serenity Prayer: 23rd Psalm for Busy People** by Jewel Diamond Taylor | 120 |
| **The Wind of Change** by Stephanie J. Gates | 123 |
| **Basking in the Beauty of Life** by Valorie Burton | 127 |

## *JOURNEY TO SUCCESS AND PROSPERITY*

| | |
|---|---|
| **The Color of Light** by Sandra M. Yee | 133 |
| **Freedom and Feasts** by Maria Denise Dowd | 139 |
| **Twenty-one** by Doreene Hamilton | 149 |
| **Power of the Pixie** by Rhonda Kuykendall-Jabari | 154 |
| **Life Savers Come in Red and Green** by Maria Denise Dowd | 159 |
| **A Higher Plateau** by Gequeta Valentine | 163 |
| **Seeds for Abundance** by Shu Oce Ani | 166 |
| **A Woman's Treasures** by Ann Clay | 169 |
| **Rivers of Abundance** by Rafiki Cai | 171 |
| **Praise and Prosperity for the Priestesses** by Sandra M. Yee | 178 |

# Journey To Faith And Spirituality

*I delight in an endless spiritual quest to know myself and to unfold the mysteries of reality.*
—Queen Reverend Mutima Imani

# *Perfectly Divine Mates*

## By Kamilah Hasan

*Out of her primordial waters*
*He came*

*He came willing and able*
*Willing and able to make manifest whatever SHE desired*
*Making their union higher than any other*

*They love the many ways they can make each other feel*
*Uncovering all that is real, they are*
*Perfectly Divine Mates*

*Who make the Universe go round*
*They found*
*They discover*
*Their completion*
*Through the synergy of their*
*Masculine and feminine energies*
*Balanced in Harmony*

*Never forgetting that WE*
*Always subdue I*
*So they fly in the cosmos of love*
*Above all limitations*
*To be their fate*

*Who no longer place themselves before each other*
*Because they love each other*
*For the reason that they can make each other feel*
*Real gooood, on the inside*
*Can't run, can't hide*
*From that tingling sensation*
*That makes ya head pop off!*
*Lost, in eternal bliss*
*Sealed with a kiss, they are*
*Perfectly Divine Mates*

*Who shall still meet with challenges*
*Obstacles placed for one's spiritual evolution*
*They will always formulate the correct solution*
*As they search within*
*Look deep within their hearts*
*To the essence of Self*
*In order to help keep their union intact*

*They act with selflessness*
*Unselfishly they pacify*
*The ego's desperate attempt to*
*Always control and fix the situation*
*That inevitably causes confrontation and*
*Breeds barriers for stagnation*
*Yet they overcome all hindrances thrown at their relation*
*So they can continue on . . .*

*While her womb produces conscious daughters reborn*
*And his seeds grow righteous men*
*Defeating sin by upholding*
*Greatness*
*And from this we receive*
*Truth and Order*
*They live the Laws of Maat*
*Clearing clots that cloud the mind*
*Enjoying all the time spent together*
*This very precious, present moment*
*Stress free!*
*We have*
*Perfectly Divine Mates*

*Who take into their union individual gifts and talents*
*Strengths and weaknesses*
*That merge into a journey of one*
*Toward spiritual growth*

*May you grow in Peace and Light!*
*May you grow in Peace and Light!*

# *Getting There*

## By Maria Denise Dowd

There was something almost too familiar about his e-mail message. It was brief, yet oblique. There was an understated hint of expectation, but veiled in decorum. The *underlinings* of his words raised an eyebrow. I vaguely remembered his features from the week past: gentle and agile, gracious and unmistakably enchanted by the combustion in the room that afternoon. I read all of these things and felt an acquaintance of spirit. Still, I wondered, had he wandered in accidentally? A quick exchange determined otherwise.

He was positioned front row, center. I hadn't pondered long as to why no one sat closer to him. Folks often avoid filing into the seats closest to the teacher. And in church, the front row is reserved for the elders. Everyone knows this. No one sat to his left or right. Even in this modest setting, the man was an island. Front row, center.

As I presented my case before this audience of a few guests and several trainees, my playful overtures were meant to engage him... and them. He'd later ask for greater clarity, curious about any misconstrues.

Hopeful in his eyes?

Perhaps.

Although today, there is greater ambiguity in my mind's eye as to where my intuitive compass was guiding me. There was something proverbial about his nature.

That was our one and only tête-à-tête before his request for, and my delivery of, a business card into his slender fingers. He had a rough and tumbled look about him. I was lifted by his poise and it carried me out of the door as I headed for the airport. However, he didn't cross my mind for days following.

And then the e-mail arrived on an early Friday afternoon. As I fixed my eyes to read the allusion behind his words, déjà vu stroked my interiors. While he was offering some technical advice about one thing or another, a side comment caught my eye. I scrolled to find a contact number, but there was none. So I shot him an e-mail back.

The phone rang.

"Blessings and peace, Maria."

His quiet voice was punctuated with the sound of a huge smile. I answered in a tone that harmonized with his. My smile was equally weighty. We spoke of Web sites, e-mail challenges, and other biographical stuff with a clear technological slant. His passion, my lifeline. My thorn, his solutions.

His next offerings—as innocent as they were—unraveled me. One reminded me of how much time had lapsed in my quest to simply *be* me, while the other struck a note so deep, it momentarily padlocked my throat and summoned tears to my eyes. How long had it been since anyone had considered asking a question of *me* that required a pure, conscious search of my soul, without agenda or premeditation? *And* expected me to verbalize it? It was an overwhelming proposition because of those things that had transpired a thousand years back: a medley of past hurts experienced by me and hurts experienced by others that I'd had a hand in.

He was simply offering a business model that would be rooted in organic substance, rather than convention. However, his words prompted slides from a chilling yesteryear to flash through my brain, slides depicting a time when things had fallen completely apart and everyone was left disagreeing to disagree. The end results were impassable, unspeakable communication gaps and horrendous assumptions about things that weren't remotely life-threatening.

Good grief. I'd simply invited him to provide me with a proposal of possible technical services he'd render, and he slid the invitation back to me and asked me to give *him* a proposal. Immediately, I wanted to end this exercise. In my observations and experiences, when left up to their own human-riddled devices, *never* have two or more parties used the same stick to measure value. *Always* have circumstances ended painfully screwed up. One, both, or all parties feel slighted, used, or abused, hence the alarming rates of divorce and lawsuits, at least in California. I simply wanted him to lay all of his cards on the table, affording me the much easier task of saying 'yea,' 'nay,' or negotiating a middle ground. Forget the macrobiotic guesswork. All I wanted was the skinny.

Not so.

The brother was calling for a homecoming, for a return to *the Way* of the ancients.

But even our ancestors battled. And often there was bloodshed. I'd seen it with my own two eyes. I've lived through things that fell *all the way* apart.

"But why does it have to be that way?"

"Just tell me what you feel your services are worth."

"Tell me what they are worth to you."

"I don't want to do this."

"Tell me how come."

I felt drained and defeated.

"I really don't want to do this," I whispered.

Silence.

I wanted out, to curl up on my bed and rest.

He graciously changed the subject . . . then stepped unflinchingly into my private life with a seemingly loaded question.

"If you were to give yourself a nickname . . . of your choosing . . . what would it be?"

My first reaction was the cursory "I don't know." Then I remembered the very day that I *had* given it some consideration. It was several years back, during a retreat on the island of St. Kitts.

"Wild Chile," I recalled.

Naturally, he laughed and affirmed that the name suited me.

Naturally, I thought that all men would say that.

The next two hours were a complete blur.

"Come take me away," I remembered typing into the e-mail's subject line. I hesitated for a few seconds, but it didn't stop me from clicking Send.

Wild Chile.

The next two hours, more blur.

I understood perfectly why I was in my prized, auction-scored 1979 avocado-green Mercedes 240 diesel headed north on Highway 5.

He spoke of *providence* and it came from the core, a place of unequivocal knowing.

I trusted my instincts and where my entire life was headed.

With a cynical eye, the scrutinizer would have screamed, "Woman, are you nuts?"

However, to this peculiarly insightful s*alvaje* eye (fairly fluent in Spanish, he took it upon himself to add more spice to the nickname game), I *knew* I was on a path that was headed toward a new rising sun.

Over the next thirty-six hours, we *quantum-leapt* through the clouds on a direct course to *Ra*, so brilliant that it made us lightheaded and drenched with the sweat of our masterful minds. From the gray vapors arose a magnificent *Prosperity Journey*, birthed from hours and hours of acumen, reflection, and remembrance. During

*Journey to Faith and Spirituality*

this intensive moment of time, our prosperity journey grew a mind, heart, legs, arms, eyes, feet, and a soul. Its foundation spanned the continents, seasons, ancient times, and light-years, rooted in a new kind of faith, finely blended with deep adoration, potential, and commitment. Yes, two like minds could reignite fires of passion, promise, and prosperity. From exercises of recollection, deliberation, acceptance, and mutual respect grew a masterpiece.

Today, we speak of *Spiritual Oneness*, a place where men and women can evolve to, a place where vows transcend the madness created by mythologies that never even belonged to us.

By working our energies collectively, due-diligently massaging out the kinks of our past raw dealings, and moving into a space that's organic, loving, intimate, principled, disciplined, open, and honest, more of us will reach that moment in the sun of abundance and prosperity.

It's time for us to remember *the Way*, to reconnect, celebrate, and create positive energy flow, love, and true intimacy. And it's time for us to reclaim *our* rites and rituals. Yes, those belong to us.

This essay is dedicated to my Friend in Life, who took me away, kept me safe, and transported me back more inspired, mindful . . . and ready.

# Tête-à-tête

## By Rafiki Cai

I sat there gazing at the e-flyer that a new colleague had sent me. It spoke of a Warm Spirit event to be held in Oakland, with two keynote speakers. One was the founder of African American Women on Tour. I immediately did a check on the Warm Spirit organization, because I had never heard of it before. I liked the Web site, and at first was energized as I reasoned that this was a black-owned company. When I researched a bit further, and found that the company was headquartered in Clackamas, Oregon, I kind of said to myself, "Oh well. That's interesting." Despite my findings, I still felt drawn to attend the event.

My soul was due for some good energy. I had been marooned in Silicon Valley for weeks, trying to finish a project that was beginning to feel like my own Afghanistan. The night before, my laptop—considered a techie's Uzi—had been stolen, along with an Armani suit. Yes. This black man needed to be in the presence of some dynamic personalities, to be lifted and engaged. No matter what, I resolved,

I'd be in Oakland, and I'd come expecting to be inspired, even if I couldn't be most dapper in my favorite suit.

The nature of the event had not been thoroughly explained to me. So when I stepped into a gathering of all black women, all scurrying about pampering stations, lit candles, and rows of self-care products, I said to myself, "Wow." I was in the company of my sisters. My eyes drifted around the room, taking in all the faces and smiles. My soul soaked up the vibration of it all. I was asked whose guest I was, and in time was introduced to my host, whom I had not met before. She was rather busy coordinating details of the event, and so I found my way around the products, pampering stations, and other guests while we waited for the actual program to commence.

Of course, I noticed her, even in spite of all the other beautiful and dynamic sisters in the room. That hair. That free, natural, speaks-of-confidence hair. I had just recently shaved off seventeen years of locks, and so that hair had a pronounced impact on me. Eventually, I introduced myself. Our exchange was cordial, but brief. I looked forward to hearing her speak later. I had no idea of what those later moments would actually hold.

Of course, I sat in the front. From childhood I had been trained to sit nowhere else. As an adult, the habit had carried forth mostly out of always wanting to get the best of what was being offered; to be visible and accessible to the presenter, during and after a presentation. She brought warmth to the floor. She was informative, energetic, and she made the audience laugh. She was good. I sat giving my full attention, as did others. I was also mindful to take written notes on the business elements of her comments. Then it all began: my tumble into the hole toward Wonderland.

She came and stood right near me, and began to make references about me right in the middle of her presentation. "I can tell this brother knows something about the laying on of hands." I was absolutely dazed. This woman was strong, bold, and smooth. I squirmed a bit from the glare of the spotlight. It was a small gathering. I was the only man present. Now, I would be lying if I said that the attention, though a bit embarrassing, wasn't a part of what I had come for. A side of me cautioned me not to read too much into the comment. It had just been a ploy to move the energy of the entire gathering, not just me, my inner voice counseled. Even if that were true, it had touched me nonetheless.

After the speaking portion of the program, she seemed continuously engrossed in a conversation with the other speaker, also a very dynamic and successful sister in the Warm Spirit family. I watched from afar as they laughed, embraced, exchanged. I was glad for them. Two powerful sisters were building their bonds and exploring the bridges between their resources and efforts. I dared not to interrupt in any way. So it was not until the very end of the event that I was able to get a word in and secure a business card. I tucked it away, resolving that I'd contact her soon. For years I had attempted to get our consulting firm on her radar. How the desires of our heart painstakingly, but surely, wind their way.

Despite the "laying on of hands" blurb, I was cautious and slow in reaching out. I went to her Web site and read that she had a "partner." How could she not? I reasoned. Oh well. That's the way of the world. I perused her site, making notes of a few technological things. After a while, though, my fingers were drawn to the keyboard. I fired off an e-mail offering my observations. As I hit the Send button, I was hopeful, not out of disregard or disrespect for the brother that had been referred to on her site, but just out of a sense of "hope against hope." This woman was a light, an achiever, a free spirit. How could I not hope?

I sat there realizing that it was Friday afternoon. She might not actually read my e-mail until Monday morning, at the earliest. I'd just have to be patient. Just as I had resolved myself to this possibility, the little sky-blue window in the lower left corner of my screen signaled me that I had mail. She was responding already. Here was someone who also spent considerable time at the keyboard. I smiled inside. She was a woman after my own heart. The e-mail bore her phone numbers and an invitation to call. I took a deep breath and dialed. The conversation flowed amazingly well. Of course, the icebreaker was the discussion of technology matters, but quickly our conversation flowed into more charged waters.

She wanted a quote for services, which was reasonable enough in the general scheme of things. However, I was tired of the "general scheme of things." I had been down this road with many a national leader and organizations. I wanted to see and experience something different. I wanted to encounter a person's ability to assess, appreciate, and honor value and quality. I wanted no more of hiding behind the protocols of the marketplace, formalities, and numbers on paper. If what was in our hearts was pure, then it had a rightful and visible place in business, a central one in fact. Establishing our own culture of commerce along these lines would pave a way toward our finding renewed integrity between ourselves and would unlock an important pathway to the incalculable riches within each of us.

Though she could grasp what I was espousing, she couldn't so abruptly make the transition, not in just one sitting. I understood. Though it didn't have to be resolved right now, I was adamant about my position. We shifted to other channels in the water, and before we knew what had hit us, we were flying down some pretty powerful rapids. The gate to those waters seemed to be the question: "If you could choose a nickname for yourself, what would it be?" The inquiry was an attempt to see how she saw herself, or the internal vision of the person she really wanted to be. I was tickled, but not totally surprised by her answer, "Wild Chile." She knew who she was. She was connected to who she wanted to be and she was being it, wearing it, and now even saying it. This was good.

If something is important to us, we should learn to speak it in multiple languages, to ring it more clearly on the waves of existence. Believing this, my immediate impulse was to give her my loose Spanish interpretation—(*Mujer*) *Salvaje*. I pledged to let that be my salutation to her, a simple way of supporting and saluting her vision of herself. From there, the floodgates flew open even wider. I tempted her with an invitation to be "benignly kidnapped."

"I can be kidnapped," she quickly responded. My heart pounded. Before we could abscond, there were things she needed to check on to ensure their order. We agreed that we'd reach back for each other at a set time.

I was excited. Overwhelmed. Uplifted. Encouraged. I had needed and acted, and true to its nature, *the Oneness* had responded accordingly. After what seemed a short eternity, I dialed her back. My ears were met with "Come take me away." Wow. Life is still capable of unfolding dreams. As I traveled to our meeting point, I knew I was journeying into transformation. I was stepping through a portal that opened into the life that I had yearned for, felt destined for. It was happening. I saw it. I was redeeming the prayers and faith of the many who had lifted me up as "one of the ones."

Our weekend together was amazing. It was abundant in multiple ways. We had intentionally chosen a waterfront retreat, but we never made it down to the water. That, in and of itself, was profound, seeing that we both love the water. The energy inside our cocoon was so intense, so nurturing. We felt emotion at the speed of blood flow. We brainstormed at the speed of light. We saw the path in front of us and embraced it quicker than the speed of either blood or light. Being afraid never entered our minds.

Believe in love. It is the fount of abundance, and it can flow in our lives, but only where our courage and action make space for it. Don't allow your inner hearing or sight to be barred from recognizing it when it stands before you. And, by all means, keep showing up in the quality spaces and places where it's likely to be in attendance. One of these days, if it hasn't already happened, love is going to be there for you, and your life will never be the same.

Tête-à-tête implies heart-to-heart, and describes that deep, soulful connection that two or more people who walk in faith and truth experience. Describe your divine-right partner or friend in living color and with the fullest of your creative expression. . . .

# Retreat, Reflect, and Advance

## By Caroline Shola Arewa

Fear is the number-one obstacle on the path to success. As an international speaker and success coach, I work with many different people. Yet the same issue always comes up—fear, that feeling we get that makes us freeze inside. There is a story told in India of a woman walking home on a cold dark night. On her path, she sees a snake and is so terrified that she refuses to take another step on her journey. Her friend walks up to the snake and on closer inspection realizes that it is merely a piece of curled-up rope, yet it prevented the woman from moving forward. Of course she is immediately reassured when told there is nothing to fear.

How often has this happened to you? How often have you allowed fear to stop you in your tracks, only to realize that all was safe and secure? Illusions take shape in our minds. This fear, or False Evidence Appearing Real, allows paralysis to set in.

I think stress diminishes during the summer months and fear takes a short sabbatical. The sun's warmth creates expansion and openness. We slow down a bit, as the sun begs us to relax and enjoy. We look up more. With our heads raised, we can actually see people passing by. We smile and laugh more. There is more ease. Things are nice and familiar. We feel good and act accordingly. The sun seems to bring out the best in us.

So what happens as the sun closes in on us and the nights grow ever dark? Does it mean that we must also contract and close down? Must we embrace stress again and walk with our heads down, protected against the elements? It's not compulsory to be cold, distressed, and stressed in autumn or winter once we come to accept that contraction is a natural process. All life expands and contracts, opens and closes. Day becomes night and night becomes day. Summer falls into winter. Spring opens into summer. It's natural law. And we, as humans, are part of the universal scheme of things. We are not outside nature and its rhythms. So it is quite likely that as the weather gets colder, we too close in.

And, although by nature's design we contract into the cold winter months, it's not a signal to ignore passersby on the street or to stop laughing and become fearful. Instead, it's a time to recharge our internal batteries. It is a time to retreat into a sort of hibernation.

Retreat has nothing to do with defeat. It's not a fear-based backward step. Rather, it's preparation for making an advance. Retreats provide space for self-regulation. Each night we silently retreat from the world. We sleep and renew our energy for the coming day. The mind works through the day's challenges and energy flows more freely, enhancing our health.

At times we need spiritual retreats, special spaces where we can reconnect with our Creator and the rhythms of life. At least twice a year, we need to take a few days away from everything to reflect on what is really important to us. We need a place where we can reassess what we are creating in our lives, to ask ourselves, "Am I living the life of my dreams or is success escaping me?"

Your wildest dreams are often a glimpse at your divine purpose. Yet, fear can strangle our dreams. We're all here for a reason and that is to fulfill part of the divine plan. We need time to reflect, time to nurture ourselves and relax in natural surroundings. We need space to pray, meditate, and refocus. Such times help us face fear, reduce stress, and establish balance and success in our lives.

Being in nature is very healing and helps us to realign with the natural order of things. Water, mountains, and the vast green wilderness are all places of beauty and harmony. Prayer and meditation go hand in hand. Prayer is speaking to God and meditation is listening to the reply. Just as we pray daily, we also need longer times away from everything where we can pray and meditate to help erase the fears that block our path.

Faith is the perfect antidote to fear. Knowing that even in the most difficult times we can hold on to a vision and have faith that our chal-

*Journey to Faith and Spirituality*

lenges will be overcome. When we have faith, fear still shows up on our path. However, we recognize it immediately and are not paralyzed by its presence. Instead, we successfully move forward, knowing that all is well. That's the distinction. We enjoy peace of mind when we ask for assistance in all of our endeavors. Pray every day to create ease. This way you can embrace success in every step. If you are ready to claim your success without stress, give yourself time to Retreat, Reflect, and Advance.

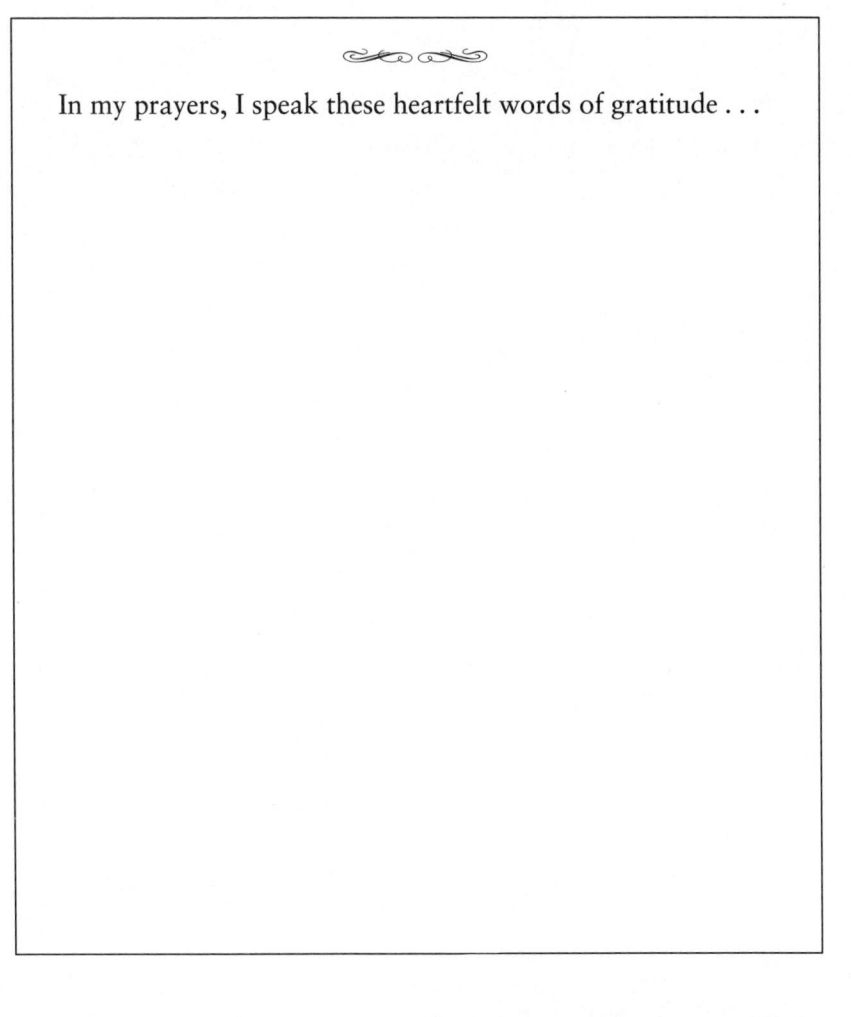

In my prayers, I speak these heartfelt words of gratitude . . .

*Journey to Faith and Spirituality*

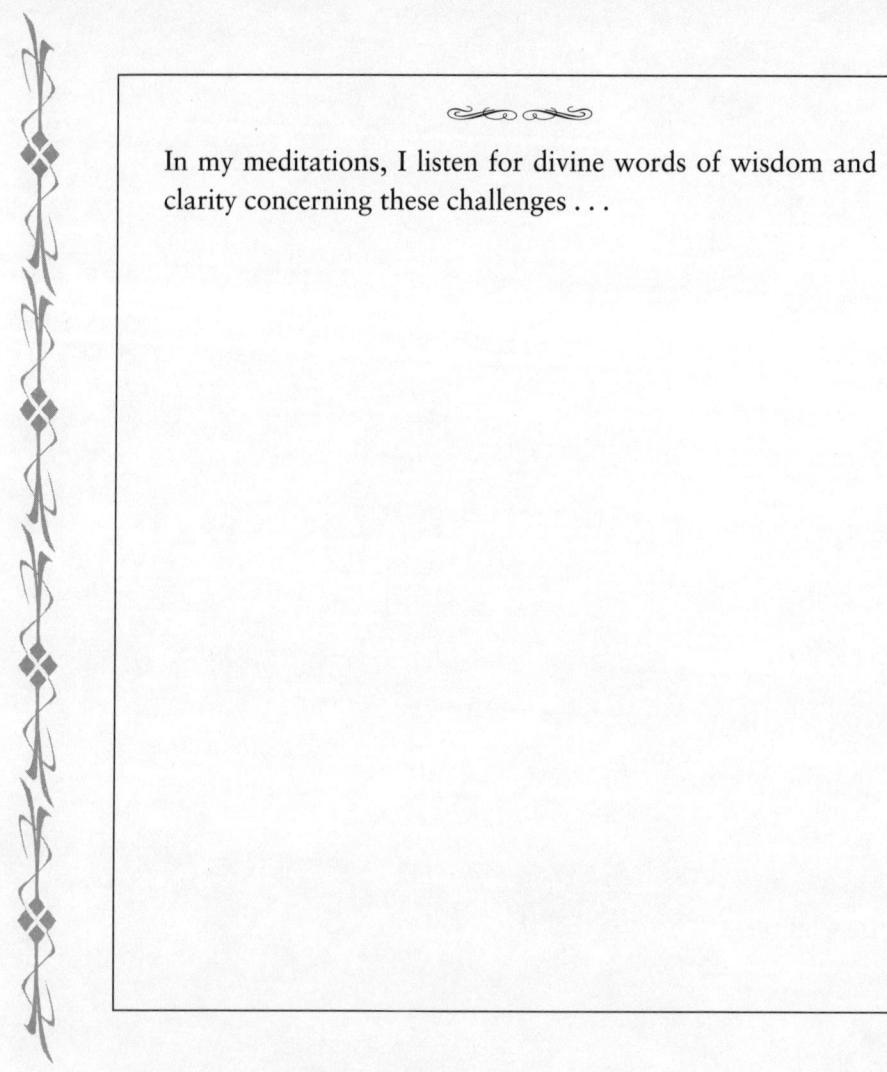

In my meditations, I listen for divine words of wisdom and clarity concerning these challenges . . .

# *Just for Today*

## By Reverend Victoria Lee-Owens

*Just for today, I will hold no fear. And when tomorrow comes, it will be today and again, I will hold no fear.*

# *Journey to Healing*

## By Carolyn Ross

In moments of desperation and dark awakening, one is more available and more alive than at any other time in life. When these moments occur, there is a sense of great possibility as the layered barriers of past experiences, emotions, and fears are forcibly stripped away like the bark of a tree. Underneath, while raw, wounded feelings are revealed, the desire for life is omnipresent.

I've heard it said that everyone, at some time, faces a "dark night of the soul." This phrase was coined by the Spanish mystic St. John of the Cross, whose life of suffering led him to a deeper level of contemplation of the divine, and then to enlightenment. When I faced my own dark night, I was not unaware of this notion that struggle precedes an opening of one's consciousness. In the meantime, I wondered, wasn't there an easier way? I had experienced this sacred space as a doctor, vicariously through my patients, when I stood at the door to that darkness but did not enter.

During my twenty years of practicing medicine, there were many patients whose stories touched my life. In many ways, their stories were healing salve to my own personal wounds or shed light on problems I faced in my own life. It always seemed that waves of a certain problem came through the office during the exact same time period that I faced similar situations. For this reason, I often thought of my patients as my own personal team of angels. This scenario was magnified in an unexpected way when I sold my practice to spend more time with my son and pursue other creative goals.

I set about "recovering" from twenty years in a hectic, demanding, and increasingly stressful profession. Little did I know that this would be the end of my ability to practice medicine, if not forever, at least in the foreseeable future.

Two months before I sold my practice, I contracted a viral infection that settled with a vengeance in my lungs. After two courses of a strong antibiotic, I was still coughing and felt tired all the time. Several weeks later, I developed a second episode of what seemed to be the same infection. I chalked it up to stress and the long hours I was working. I looked forward to the future when I would be able to rest and work part-time, perhaps even take a vacation.

However, six months later, I was still not feeling well. I suffered from pain in my muscles and joints, extreme fatigue, headaches, difficulty sleeping through the night, trouble concentrating, and memory loss. Eventually, I was diagnosed with chronic fatigue and immunodeficiency syndrome (CFIDS). At the time in my life when I should have been having fun, released from the burden of running a large

*Journey to Faith and Spirituality*

medical practice, able to spend more time with my son and pursue my dream of writing a book, my life was turned upside down.

For months, I could do little besides get my son off to school and pick him up at the end of the day. The time in between, I spent in bed. My nights were literally nightmarish, as I tossed and turned, trying to go to sleep despite the pain in most of my body, then waking up in the early morning hours, struggling to go back to sleep.

At the time of my diagnosis, I recalled a favorite patient of mine, who had CFIDS. She was a young lawyer at the beginning of a very promising career when she was diagnosed. She was engaged to be married the following year. She was very active in sports, including hiking, skiing, and surfing. Within a year of her diagnosis, she had to quit practicing law, lost her fiancé, and was unable to pursue any of her former activities. She was at her lowest point, taking turns sleeping at one friend's house and then moving on to the next friend, so as not to wear out her welcome.

As I pondered my own fate, I thought of my patient and knew that I was in for the fight of my life, just as she had been. I remembered the times she sat in my exam room and we discussed her options for living arrangements, while I tried to help her find treatments for her symptoms. I remembered the battle she had in getting disability payments because of the type of diagnosis she had. I remembered how sensitive she was to even the smallest dose of any medication and how careful I had to be when prescribing something for her. I remembered how she was deserted by some of her friends who could not go the distance with her during her illness. In remembering, I had to thank her for teaching me skills that I would now need to practice in my own life.

So began my journey to healing that forced me to question all that I held true about medicine, healing, and life itself. My colleagues in conventional medicine had little to offer me except strong and debilitating painkillers, muscle relaxers, and antidepressants. These medications all made my memory worse and made the fog that had shrouded my brain since the beginning of this mystifying illness even thicker. Many days I felt as if I were a zombie—trying to get from one task to another until I could go back to bed. I was filled with guilt about not being able to do more with my son. My illness and the reaction people had to it ("You don't look sick") caused me to withdraw from many of my friends and activities. The pain made me irritable and immobile. Worst of all was my difficulty with thinking. As a doctor, I'd always been very proud of my quick mind. Well, "pride comes before the fall" was a phrase that echoed many times in that now dulled and confused mind.

I knew that CFIDS was called the "invisible illness." This is a category of diseases for which there is no specific medical regimen or cure. People with these diseases can look perfectly normal while feeling quite ill. Other invisible illnesses include the "Gulf War syndrome," fibromyalgia, depression, lupus, hepatitis, multiple chemical sensitivities, neurasthenia, and chronic migraine headaches. Often patients with these diseases aren't taken seriously by friends and family because they don't appear to be sick. There are usually no lab tests or X-rays that can prove the diagnosis. Therefore, they are diagnosed by exclusion—physicans exclude what patients don't have, then infer from their symptoms which disease they do have. This lack of visual or test proof creates a bias among some physicians, who think these invisible illnesses are "all in the patient's head." Insurance companies use this bias to deny claims, thereby adding to the burden of illness the need to fight for one's livelihood. Even though I was a physician, I experienced many instances of being disbelieved by other physicians I sought out for care. There were some who blatantly told me they thought I was just "acting sick" to get out of working. This and my own discomfort created a resolve not to complain or ask for help—the exact opposite of the lesson I was to learn very soon. I came to admire people like my patient, who persisted despite their illness. I wondered how Laura Hillenbrand had been able to write *Seabiscuit* when I found it difficult to write just a page in my journal each day. I knew why Michelle Akers wanted to continue her soccer career, as I continued practicing tae kwon do despite the pain. It was the only thing I had to show as an accomplishment during this time.

Finally, in a desperate search for anything that would help me feel better, I turned to alternative therapies, and through these I found the true meaning of my journey.

It started during a session of Phoenix Rising Yoga, when I felt a flood of overwhelmingly intense emotions. A dark abyss of sadness welled up from somewhere deep inside me. Tears flooded my cheeks. Next, I felt as if I was suffocating. With a change in positions, I saw a blinding pale yellow light—the brightest light I had ever seen. Within this floodlight, I felt immense love surrounding me and enormous peace and joy. Then I heard a voice in my mind that said, "Know that I am with you. I have been with you since before your birth and am with you now." I cried tears of relief and joy. I knew I had experienced something divine. It was not within my scientific medical training to understand it. Indeed, I could not bring myself to even talk about it. But the experience pointed me in a direction that paralleled my quest for physical healing.

This experience early in my illness set me on a spiritual search for meaning. While I continued to search for therapies to ease the pain and help me sleep or think better, I also knew that the higher purpose of my journey, for me, was one of spiritual healing, something I would not necessarily have known or thought I needed. However, the desire was intense and I could not keep myself away from it, whatever "it" was.

On the physical side, some of my symptoms improved with acupuncture and various forms of energy healing. I tried Chinese herbs, which decreased the constant stomach upsets I had. I learned to treat myself with Reiki and, to my surprise, it helped me sleep better. During the first year after my diagnosis, I had several relapses that consisted of high fevers, flulike symptoms, increasing fatigue, and unbearable pain. They lasted from days to weeks, and I was always left frightened by the severity of the episodes. Because of decreased general physical activity, I gained more than twenty pounds. I continued to exercise as much as possible, but at a much decreased rate than before. I tried changes in my diet, supplements, and herbs, with little effect on either my weight or my symptoms. I began to realize that my situation was not going to improve overnight, as I had secretly hoped, and so I had to make accommodations. I had to surrender to the disease, at least for now, rather than continuing to wage a losing battle.

So, for the first time in my life, I gave in. When I felt tired, I took naps. Spending time with my son now took the form of reading in bed or watching movies on television rather than kicking a soccer ball in the park or playing mentally challenging games, such as chess, with him. Trying to keep his life somewhat normal, on days when I felt better, I took the opportunity to invite his friends over to play with him or swim in our backyard pool. In turn, I built credits with the other moms. When I wasn't feeling well, I could count on them to have him over to play at their house, giving me much needed rest time.

I began to meditate. Through this I connected with God and could feel the calmness of Spirit settle and guide me. This led me to different healers who helped me improve my symptoms. I also did a series of yoga exercises at bedtime that helped with the pain. More and more, I looked inside myself to see what needed healing. I used the book *The Artist's Way* as a means to start journaling again. The "morning pages" revealed my interior landscape and allowed me to examine and explore it more fully.

During this time, I met other people who, like myself, realized that their illness was a call to take spiritual action. One woman, the wife of a physician, developed a life-threatening form of psoriatic arthritis that almost caused her to be wheelchair-bound. While waiting for her managed care company to approve her visit to a rheumatologist, she tried vitamins and supplements. Within weeks, she began to recover and by the time she saw the specialist, she opted not to take the drugs he offered. Instead she stayed with her own regimen. When I saw her she had cured herself of all symptoms, with the exception of small skin patches of psoriasis that broke out during stressful times. She had also learned to appreciate life's blessings more and to take time out for herself, rather than always being a giver to others.

I met another woman who used a form of meditation to heal specific problems. While her physician had strongly recommended that she have a liver transplant for the "worst case of hepatitis" he had ever seen, despite her fears, she used the technique to heal herself.

*Journey to Faith and Spirituality*

When I met her, she had had normal liver function tests for more than two years. She'd also learned forgiveness and how to let go of anger. Her own experience with the isolation during her illness enabled her to understand the clients in her counseling practice, many of whom were experiencing similar challenges.

My encounters with these women and others inspired me to follow my own *small, still voice of intuition* and find my own path to healing. As well, they reaffirmed for me that spiritual healing goes hand in hand with physical healing.

At present, I've made progress in both the physical and spiritual arenas. However, the journey is not complete. During the past two years, I've learned to find and follow my own truth. I've begun to dream again of accomplishments I might still make, something, at one point in time, I found despairing. I have lost many friends, but made many more new ones. My new friends are solid, real people who support me fully. And I now feel deserving of that support and can accept their help.

No longer standing alone as an independent woman, I now allow others to give to me, and I accept all gifts graciously and gratefully. My gratitude for all things of beauty and joy has expanded tremendously. I love the flowers in my yard, my son's beautiful smile and quick wit, the sunny days, and the sound of rain on my patio. I appreciate days when I can be physically active, taking a walk or playing catch. I continue to find teachers and other earth angels on my path, and they enrich my life in untold ways. Beyond all of this is my close abiding relationship with Spirit that has sustained me through the dark nights and the days of despair and has taught me no matter how things look on the surface, "All is well."

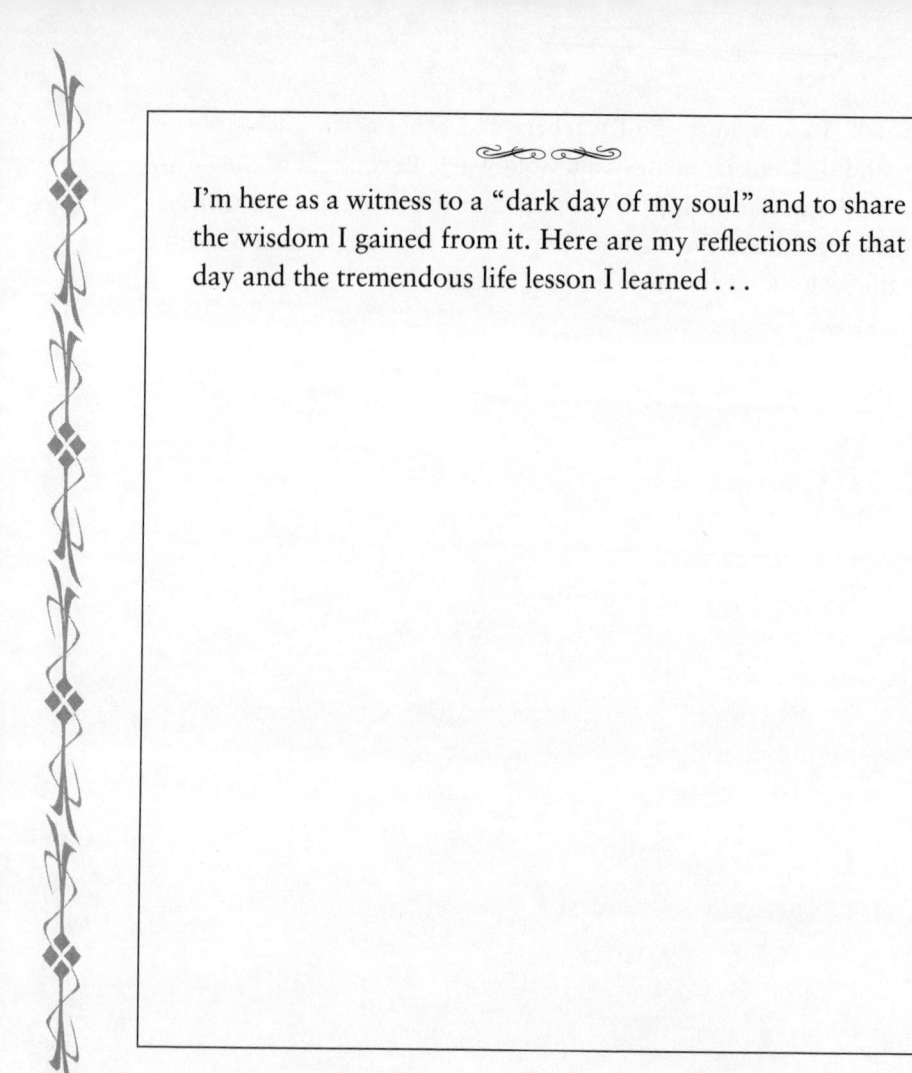

I'm here as a witness to a "dark day of my soul" and to share the wisdom I gained from it. Here are my reflections of that day and the tremendous life lesson I learned . . .

# The Other Side of the Canyon

## By Chanequa Walker-Barnes

There is a Native American proverb that says, "As you go the way of life you will see a great chasm. Jump. It is not as wide as you think." The chasm is what separates who we are from who we wish to be. On the side we stand upon, there is the safety and comfort of being on familiar ground. We know this territory. We have lived here for a long time, maybe all of our lives. We have prepared ourselves to be here and now know the lay of the land so well that we could traverse it blindfolded.

And we are not alone on this side. We have plenty of company—friends, family, colleagues—living here with us and helping us to remain content on our side of the canyon. Some of them are genuinely concerned about our well-being. They worry about what might happen to us if we choose to make the jump. Others are not so well intentioned. They want us to remain where we are because our doing so validates their decision to do the same.

Sometimes people succeed in convincing us that life will be too difficult on the other side of the canyon and we settle back into our comfort zone. But other times, they are not as successful. Try as they may, they cannot still that quiet, yet persistent, voice of discontent that emanates from within our souls—the voice that tells us that there is something more waiting for us on the other side of the canyon. It may be a new relationship, a new job or career path, or a new outlook on life. It may be a chance at greater happiness, freedom, financial prosperity, peace, or fulfilling a lifelong dream.

But getting there means leaving where we are, taking a step out of our comfort zone, and leaping across the vast chasm. It means risking the possibility of losing something—relationships, social status, material comforts. It means risking the chance of failure.

Fear of failure is what most often keeps us from making the leap. We dread failure. After all, from early childhood, we are taught that failure is the opposite of success. As students, we are measured by a grading system that ranges from excellent performance on one end to failure on the other. If we fail, we are told that it's because we did not try hard enough (or perhaps not at all) or because we are somehow deficient in our abilities. Failure is often accompanied by ridicule and shame by fellow students and maybe even by parents and teachers. Students who have the unfortunate experience of failing an entire grade often go through their entire educational experience, perhaps even their entire lives, thinking of themselves as failures. And our training in fear of failure is not limited to school. At home we learn that failing to meet the expectations or rules of our parents is accompanied by punishment that sometimes may be severe. Those who fail repeatedly are labeled "bad," "difficult," or "incorrigible." And these definitions of failure often accompany us into adulthood, even when they have outlasted their usefulness.

So as we peer across the chasm, desperately trying to glimpse the life that awaits us on the other side, we are held back by the fear of failure.

"It's too dangerous."

"I'll never make it."

"I don't have enough money."

"I don't have enough time."

"I'm not good enough."

"My family won't support me."

"I don't have the skills I need to do it."

"People will talk about me."

"I've invested too much time and energy into what I already have."

"It's better to be safe than sorry."

These things and more we tell ourselves any time we even consider the possibility of taking the leap. Instead, we look over the edge of the canyon to see whether there is a safety net in place. With none in sight, we creep back to our comfort zone. After all, it seems like the sensible thing to do.

But is it the faithful way? The faithful view of failure sees it not as the opposite of success, but as the by-product of courage. It is what happens when we approach the edge of the canyon and, trusting in the goodness of the Universe to carry us, we jump into the unknown despite our fear. The faithful know that even when we "fail," we have succeeded because we had the courage to make the leap of faith. And the faithful trust that the Creator will pick us up again, if we fail. And though we may be a bit battered and bruised at the end of the jump, the pain is only temporary. All things work together for the good of those who believe. The faithful know this and trust it wholeheartedly. They understand that failure is not a permanent outcome. It is just one more stepping stone in the adventure called life.

There are two pathways through life—the faithful way and the fearful way. They are not completely separate paths. Both curve and intersect so often that the faithful are not exempt from moments of fear and the fearful have opportunities to demonstrate their faith on a daily basis. The main difference between the roads is that the road of fear only requires us to make small steps. The road of faith, on the other hand, sometimes breaks off at the edge of a huge canyon. To continue on the path, we must take a leap. The trick is that when we take a true leap of faith, the safety net does not appear before the jump. It comes after we are already in the air. When we leap, our jump sends a shout of immense praise and trust to the Creator. And in return, the Creator provides the net.

Do you trust the Creator to provide the net? If so, what are you waiting for? There's something waiting for you on the other side of the canyon.

In this moment of retreat and reflection, I recognize that my fears are merely falsehoods that I've fostered. Today, I'm committed to relinquishing my fears. Here is how the Creator will support my journey and daring leap of faith . . .

# *And I Cried*

## By Kallene Rutherford

*Last night it rained outside*
*And I cried*
*Over my TV came the voices and screams in my head*
*Drawing me in, beckoning me to listen more closely*
*The rain fell so hard I could hear its moan upon the silvered*
  *leaves of the lilac tree*
*I paced slow*
*Last night it rained outside*
*And I cried*
*The thunder croaked*
*The tears trembled down my face*
*Steady and purposeful, fast and sure*
*The sounds grew louder and louder*
*I walked faster and faster to drown out the voices*
*Faster and faster to distribute the waves of emotion*
*My stride now matching the drumbeat of the raindrops beating*
  *down on my back*

*Porch*
*Last night it rained outside*
*And I cried*
*Phil Collins crooned out "I Wish it Would Rain Down" and I cried*
*Suddenly now angels breaking through like rays of sun through clouds*
*I opened the windows to breathe in the freshly soaked earth*
*The screaming lies, hurt, pain, and shame rolling down and pouring out into the*
*Cleansed damp air*
*Morning had arrived and it appeared I had not drowned*
*Reached for the radio to flood out the remaining dew lingering in my head from the*
*Night's hardships*
*Last night it rained outside*
*And I cried*
*But through it all I'm still here*

# *Introduction: Waiting for a Miracle*

## By Beverley East

Relationships between women are sacred and most of us have girlfriends whom we have known through high school or college, with similar interests and backgrounds that bind us together. This is a rare story of three women from totally different backgrounds. My name is Beverley East and I'm a Jamaican native who reads handwriting as a career. I've lived in more than five different countries. Ayesha Grice, a New Yorker, is an astrologist, a columnist, and a vegetarian spiritual consultant who hates to fly. And Erica Sheppard, a death row inmate, spent the early years of her life escaping abuse. Erica was raped at six, had three children by the time she was eighteen, and has never been on a train.

Our journey began four years ago. I had gone to bed with a copy of *Essence* magazine. As I was flipping through the pages and reading various articles on lifestyles and book reviews, my eyes glazed across an article entitled "Praying for a Miracle." It was about a young sister in prison. Her face could have been mine. She looked so young, so innocent. I passed the article over because I did not want to go to bed with such a heavy load on my mind. But every time I flipped the pages, the article kept resurfacing. I read it not once, but twice, and then couldn't sleep. So I got up at four in the morning and wrote to Erica Sheppard, Mountain View Prison's youngest death row inmate. I wasn't sure what to expect, but I knew that I had to reach out to her.

In New York, Ayesha Grice, who writes the astrology column for *Essence*, had also read the same article on the same night, I later learned. She decided to write to Erica as well. In fact, Erica received more than four thousand letters as a result of the article, and from all of those letters, Erica, Ayesha, and I came together.

Erica is still waiting for a retrial and every day we pray that her case will be heard. Yes, she was present at the scene of the crime, but she did not kill the woman who died. It happened in Texas.

How did Erica end up on death row?

Here is her story.

She was on the run from an abusive relationship and found shelter at her brother's house. Her brother had a white male friend staying with him, and he threatened to kill one of her children if she didn't go with him to carjack a car. Erica, not knowing what to do or where to turn, took her eight-month-old baby girl with her. The man approached a white female who, instead of handing over the keys, fought back. Erica, too frightened to run, watched as the woman was killed in front of her. The white male died two years ago in prison of AIDS and it was only after his death that Erica learned that his written statement blamed her solely for the murder. Human rights activist Bianca Jagger got involved in Erica's case. And it was Diane Weathers, the editor in chief of *Essence*, who introduced us to Erica Sheppard.

This is our journey . . . our journey of love.

# Journey to Love: the Circle of Love

## By Ayesha Grice

Love is a magnetic energy that magnifies and expands the very moment we begin to give it away. It is the force that causes us to care, to share, to forgive, to nurture others and ourselves. Love is the bond that magically draws to us good people and positive experiences. Through the law of love, everything that we need for our work and fulfillment comes to us without effort. Love energy creates unity and harmony. When love is emanating from our being, there is no room for fear, anger, anxiety, resentment, sadness, guilt, or feelings of separation. My late teacher, Isabel M. Hickey, often reminded us that at the end of our lives we'll be asked only two questions: who did you love? And, who did you help?

It was love that inspired me to write to Erica Sheppard. After reading her story in *Essence* four years ago, I wrote her a note encouraging her to stay strong and letting her know that I loved her. Then, Erica was a twenty-eight-year-old African-American woman living on death row in Texas. I didn't know what to expect when I mailed the letter, but I was pleasantly surprised when Erica wrote me back.

That was the beginning of a circle of love that continues to this day. But you need three people to make a circle. The circle was complete when I met Beverley East, a sister, an author, a graphologist from Washington, D.C. Erica was the catalyst for meeting Beverley. After writing Erica for approximately six months, she wrote me a letter saying that she wanted me to meet Beverley, who was also writing to her.

Erica said that she received more than four thousand letters as a result of the article, but decided to answer only two, Beverley's and mine. Erica explained that she viewed Beverley and me as her angels, and it was very important to her that we connect. At first I was apprehensive about meeting Beverley. What was the chance that we would even like each other? But not wanting to disappoint Erica, I agreed to meet Beverley when she came to New York as a presenter at the African American Women on Tour conference.

From our very first meeting, Beverley and I immediately bonded. We're both lap swimmers, writers, believers in positive thinking and spirituality. And our common denominator is our love for Erica Sheppard, and the great work we have to do for Erica and others who are in her situation.

And it was at our first meeting that we discovered we shared the same emotions after first reading about Erica. And while we both tried to ignore them and go to sleep, we found ourselves up at the twilight hours of the morning, writing to her.

*Journey to Faith and Spirituality*

The thing that completely amazes both Beverley and me is Erica's complete faith in God and her potential freedom. She doesn't see herself as a victim. Both Beverley and I are thankful for the presence of Erica in our lives and our friendship. Her letters from death row boost our confidence and are often intuitive and comforting. Sometimes we ask ourselves "who is this young woman who writes letters as though she knows what's going on in our lives?"

One thing I do know is that Erica and Beverley have brought more love into my life. What seemed like a selfless act of giving has actually come back to me through the law of return, tenfold. Erica and Beverley have sealed my faith in the Higher Power. They have let me know without a doubt that LOVE IS ALL THERE IS.

# *Love Is*

## By Erica Sheppard

Love is a verb—an action word, so I've been told—yet it wasn't until I experienced this "love" that I came to "know" what love truly is.

Hello there! My name is Erica Sheppard and I'd like to tell you about my Journey to Love.

In 1999, I did an interview with *Essence* magazine and I talked about some of my struggles and part of what makes me who I am today. And who am I, you may ask? I'm a survivor, a woman of courage, and a woman of faith.

In the course of this journey, I encountered two beautiful women named Beverley and Ayesha, who have become very dear friends to me. They read the article and reached out to me through letters. At first it was weird getting letters from people I didn't know, telling me that they supported me and cared about me as a person, but as we continued to write each other and learn more about each other, things began to make more sense.

By coming to know and love Ayesha and Beverley, we support and sustain each other not only through our writing, but through prayer as well. Our strong spiritual foundation helps to uphold our friendship.

Ayesha is a person of adventure. Whenever she writes, she always has an interesting story to share with me. She also has a spirit of consciousness. Wholeheartedly believing in treating people the way she wants to be treated, she gives love, and in her giving of love, it is returned to her. She believes that love is the ultimate foundation to everything created. Ayesha loves me by sharing with me and allowing me to share with her. I love her for the person she is, for the wisdom and fighting spirit she possesses and her willingness to say, no matter what, that she's here for me and she won't give up.

Beverley is a person who sees the "real you," not the person you are on the outside, but the person you are on the inside. She's gifted with the ability to see the things that you think you're hiding, and I find that intriguing. There are times I'll write her a letter and she'll write me back asking what's wrong, not because of what I've said, but because of what I haven't said. She always knows what's going on with me just by looking at my letters. Beverley loves me by showing her concern for me. I love her ability to listen and "know me."

In light of all that I've shared with you, Ayesha, Beverley, and I have never met each other face-to-face. We've exchanged photos and continue to correspond with each other. They are a blessing to me. They are my angels.

In closing, I'd like to say the most valuable lesson I have learned on this journey to love is that there are still kind, considerate, and loving people in this world who know how to reach out to others and share the greatest gift of all—the gift of love. Beverley and Ayesha, I love you and thank you for traveling on this journey with me.

Our circle will never be broken.

# A Sister-Kinda Love

## By Beverley East

The last time I loved anyone sight unseen, unknowingly, was twelve years ago, as I patiently awaited the arrival of my son. During the past four years my love for my young sisterfriend Erica has grown to be a deep love—the kind of love reserved solely for my immediate family.

Erica *is* family to me. I had no idea when I got up at four o'clock that morning to write to her that I would begin this wonderful journey of love, a journey that would profoundly and forever affect my life.

Erica is an old spirit in a young body. She has been on death row since she was nineteen years old. A great part of that time has been spent in solitary confinement. She has three children currently living with her mother in Houston. During the period when the story appeared, Erica's children were living with her ninety-year-old grandmother. How could I sleep peacefully after reading her story? How could I not respond to her needs? The *Essence* article propelled me to organize a fund-raiser and establish the Erica Sheppard Children's Trust Fund to support her three babies.

Erica has given me a new perspective on life. I whine less and I'm absolutely grateful for the smallest things I have. I now respect and understand the concept of freedom: using the phone without asking permission, fresh fruit, privacy. I'm awed by her courage, her humility, and her sharp mind. When I was sick, she sent me poems and songs that revived and comforted me. She's been my strength when I've been weak, she's been wise when I've been foolish, she's humbled me when I've been arrogant.

I reached inside to help her, but it has been her letters, her clarity, and her humor that have often sustained me on the outside. I send her postcards from every city I travel to. Sometimes I compose a short expression of love, just to let her know that I carry her in my heart.

Our circle was completed when I met Ayesha, who has supported me emotionally and spiritually. She is a calm, composed, caring warrior queen. And the circle of love continues five years later.

Three years ago, Ayesha and I finally got the chance to visit Erica at Mountain View. Meeting Erica Sheppard for the first time was an experience I will never forget. Behind those Texan bars was a queen, not a criminal; a victor, not a victim. She has survived rape, abortion, abuse, and got a stay of execution promoted by Jesse Jackson just days before she was to die.

*Journey to Faith and Spirituality*

When we met she did not complain about the injustice of an unfair trail and a poorly handled case. She did not complain about her life in prison. Instead, we talked about her life, her retrial, her future. Erica is a bright, shining star, whose spirit cannot be broken in spite of her treatment behind those Texan iron bars.

We went back to visit Erica a year later. As expected, I felt blessed and honored to be in her presence. Visitations are limited, so Erica must forgo someone else's visit to accommodate ours. She must be on her best behavior or the privilege is confiscated. So much hangs in the balance on every visit. On both occasions, we got lost, arrived late, and had to beg to be admitted. In my travels, I know that Erica keeps me in her prayers, guiding me, protecting me, keeping me safe.

Isn't love magical and magnetic? It has to be. How does a total stranger choose two people out of four thousand and create a loving circle for the three of us to share, grow, and revere? I'm still awed by Erica. Her fight has become my fight. Am I my sister's keeper? No, I am my Sister—Yes, I am.

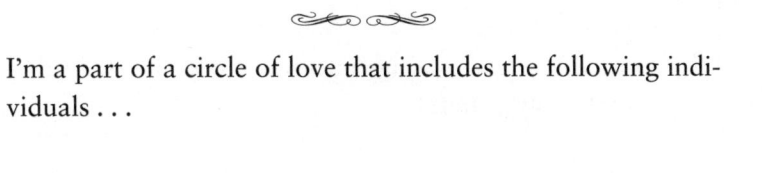

I'm a part of a circle of love that includes the following individuals . . .

*Journey to Faith and Spirituality*

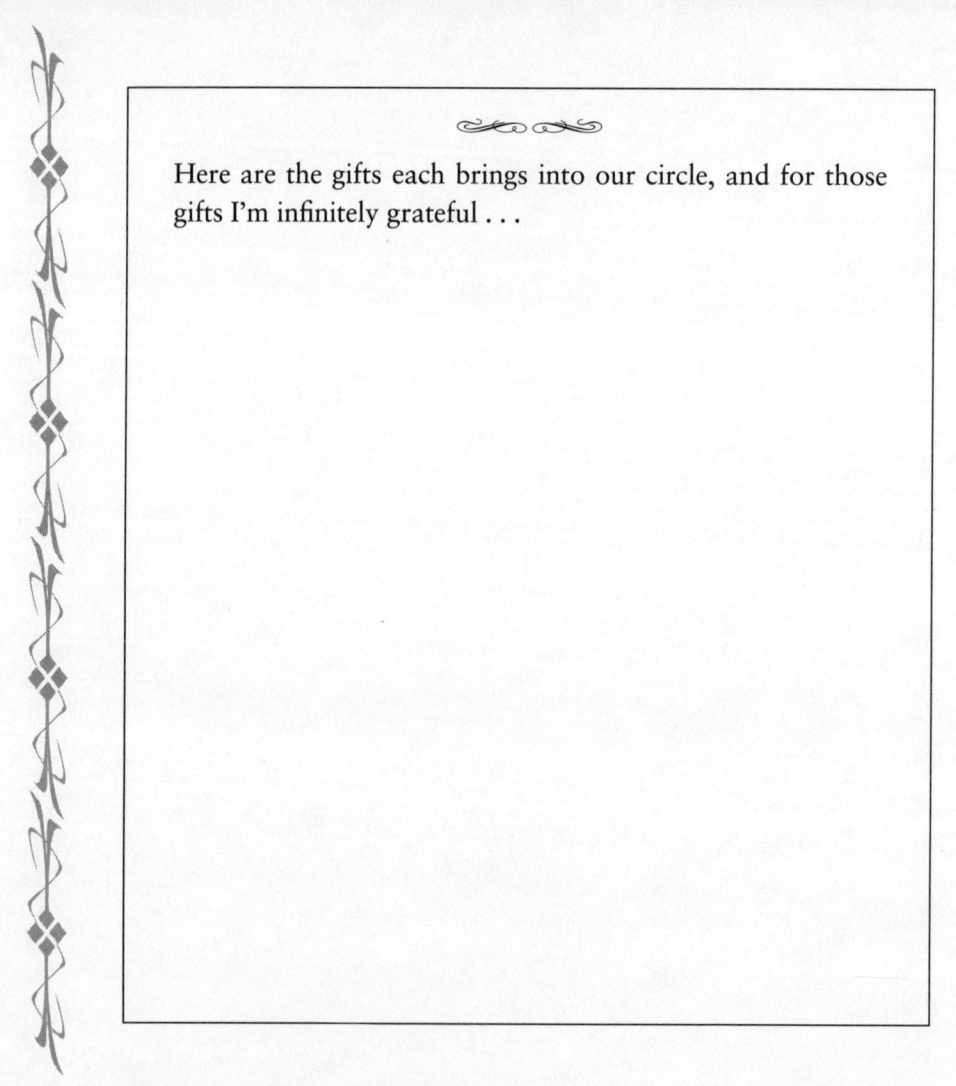

Here are the gifts each brings into our circle, and for those gifts I'm infinitely grateful . . .

# *A True Love Story*

## By Monique Brown McKenzie

When the last bell rings prior to the start of summer break, most kids breathe a sigh of relief. For me, the start of the summer was not something that I anxiously awaited. After all, I'd be shipped off to my grandmother's house in a small town in South Carolina, and that was probably the one thing I dreaded most.

My grandmother wasn't like the ones in the fairy tales. She wasn't about spoiling her grandkids by showering them with gifts and allowing them to push past the limits that are often set by stern parents. In fact, she ruled with an iron fist and didn't mind asking any of us to fetch a switch when we got out of hand. Instead of intoxicating us by the smells of fresh-baked bread and cookies, she welcomed her grandkids with the aromas of pine cleaner and laundry detergent. She ran a tight ship and I, along with my three cousins, were her mates.

Tammi was the oldest. Actually, she was only one year older than I was, but according to her, that gave her the right to step into the role as second-in-command. Whenever Grandma wasn't around, and even when she was, Tammi would spew out orders as if it was her job to keep the rest of us in check. Nikki and Kim, who were years younger, admired Tammi, and while they probably didn't like her commands any more than I did, they'd decided early on that it was better to befriend her. After all, Tammi could braid hair and if you were good to her she'd ensure that your tresses were tamed for the week. As for me, I decided to take my chances by bucking instructions. I concluded that she was a spoiled brat and refused to take heed. I also couldn't understand why the surrounding adults seemed to openly favor her. As a result, Tammi and I remained at war. That wasn't the best situation to be in, because my mom's younger siblings, who were still in the house, had made it known that Tammi was the "golden child" and anyone who didn't fall in line would feel their wrath. While Grandma never openly confirmed it, you could see that Tammi had a special place in her heart as well.

But favored or not, all of us had chores that had to be completed during the course of the day. From the time of our arrival, Grandma set the ground rules in an effort to decode us from our stay with our parents. Rule number one: "Don't let the sun hit you in the face," she'd say. That meant no matter what time you went to bed, she expected you to get up at the crack of dawn. That actually was more of a southern rule, not just hers. No matter where you laid your head on a southern pillow, folks would talk about you bad if you slept late—

and that was just past 8:00 a.m. That was a sign of laziness. So once we heard the sound of my grandmother's slippers moving about the hallway, that was our alarm clock.

First we'd make the beds, fix breakfast, wash dishes, clean up the kitchen and bathroom, and collect the clothes, hand towels, and other items for my grandmother to put in the wash. Then we'd take time out for television. "And you're not going to spend all day watching television," Grandma declared, emphasizing rule number two. So with the few hours of the day we'd have to watch television, we'd catch up on the soaps on the only TV that was made available to us. The selection was upon Tammi's insistence—of course. It didn't matter that we were no more than eleven years old, cartoons were much too childish for her. Fortunately, our daytime dramas would get interrupted at noon because that's when Grandma would insist that we go outside daily to meet the lunch truck. It was nearly torture. At the time, the area wasn't yet paved, so we had to sit out on the dirt among the raging gnats and mounting ant hills. But Grandma concluded that it was important for us to socialize with the neighborhood kids while we had sandwiches, milk, and fruit. Frankly, I'd rather have gone hungry than face the pounding heat and pesky insects, but that wasn't an option. I think our daily meeting of the lunch truck was rule number three.

After lunch, we'd usually have to hang out the items that

*Journey to Faith and Spirituality*

Grandma had washed earlier that day. Then we'd watch a few more soaps, tidy up around the house (as much as we cleaned I couldn't understand how the place always required tidying), and get ready for dinner. This led to rule number four: if you want to eat, you have to shell. So every afternoon we'd shell the peas that Grandma picked or we'd pick a few and then shell them. For some reason, we'd have to shell a new batch almost nightly. I never understood why we never had enough peas for the next day. And then if Grandma decided to make a special batch of her jelly or canned fruit or preserves, we'd have to assist with that as well by washing jars, picking fruit, or just lending a hand. After that it would be time to bring in the clothes off the line, and next we'd fold them and put them away. The wise thing to do would have been to try to do whatever task that was at hand right the first time so you could move on to something else. But I never did the wise thing. I just pretended to be wise. So my tasks usually went into overtime.

"Try it again," she'd insist as I frowned in frustration.

"That's okay," she'd say with a smile. "I have all day and I'll sit here and show you until you get it right."

And she meant exactly that. Unlike my parents, Grandma was home with us and she could focus literally all of her attention on whatever little activity was being done, even if it took several hours to complete. If I didn't wash the floor correctly, make the bed just right, or was sloppy on the folding, she'd show me how she wanted it and watch me make the adjustment—over and over again. "You can get mad at me," she stated firmly, "because I notice the angrier you get, the better you work."

Personally, I thought she was breaking a few child labor laws, but I never had the courage to tell her so. I probably wouldn't have lived long enough to talk about it. Anyway, I'd usually finish up my chores by dinner, which typically consisted of peas, rice, and the best fried chicken you ever tasted in your life, and then, if it was "Revival Time," we'd prepare for rule number five: everybody in *this* house goes to church.

*Said I wasn't gonna tell nobody but I couldn't keep it to myself.*
*Oh, I couldn't keep it to myself.*
*Said I wasn't gonna tell nobody but I couldn't keep it to myself,*
*What the Lord has done for me.*
*Has done for me.*
*You oughta been there,*
*You oughta been there,*
*When the Lord put my name on the road.*
*You oughta been there,*
*You oughta been there,*
*When the Lord saved my soul.*

Singing, clapping, dancing, shouting. Church was the only place that the adults would just let you be. Don't get me wrong, you had to be on your best behavior at church, and I got in trouble a few times for slumping in my seat or being a bit too chatty. But as long as whatever you were doing was praising the Lord, you were free.

Grandma was free, too. At times she looked like an African princess as she had her church hat propped on her head, a fan in one hand, and a Bible in the other. If I didn't know any better, I might think she was participating in her own little celebration, and maybe that *was* the case. She'd be smiling, clapping her hands, stomping her feet, and yelling things at the pastor.

"Well," she'd respond to one comment as she stood to her feet.

"Watchu say, pastor?" she'd utter at another moment.

When she finished shouting and praising, she'd take her seat with a great exhale and an "Oooh, Lawdy."

Before I knew it we'd be back home again and off to bed, and then the routine would start all over again. And that pretty much was how I saw my summer at Grandma's, and that's why I'd concluded that it was time for a change.

At age thirteen, I'd finally convinced my parents that I was old enough to make my own decisions about how I should spend my summers. I wanted to stay in New York where the action was and not in what I viewed as the backward South.

"You really don't know what you're missing," my mom said with a tear.

"Oh, but I do know," I shot back. And then the fun began. During weekends my parents would take us to Great Adventure, Coney Island, or the beach. During the week, since my parents didn't get home until about six in the evening, my brother and I pretty much had the run of the house. As long as we didn't wreck the place, my parents didn't care what we did, and my mother did all the laundry, cooking, and cleaning herself when she got home from work. We spent the entire day watching television and since there was a television in every room, we could watch whatever we wanted on two or three channels. There were no limits. We made breakfast and lunch when and if we felt like it.

"Now, this is living," I said, beaming, declaring that I had seen the last of summer visits to my grandmother's house.

From that point on, my interaction with Grandma was fairly limited. Aside from the annual birthday cards and maybe a few telephone calls, I didn't see her very much. When I did visit, it was nothing like my summer visits because my parents and my mother's siblings were around. They took care of the cooking and cleaning. We kids just observed from the sidelines and learned how to stay out of grown folks' business.

In fact the next time I got a chance to have a real chat with my grandmother was years later in a hospital. She wasn't as stern as I'd remembered. Her voice was weak and her eyes were weary. I read a Bible verse to her and reminded her that she was the one who taught it to me. I'm not sure if she truly understood me, but she smiled peacefully as she waved to some invisible angels that she said were floating around in her room.

A few weeks later, Grandma passed away. Her funeral was so packed that people were pouring out of the back of the church. I learned more about my grandmother on that day than I'd learned in my entire life. I now understood why we shelled peas every night. It seemed that our grandmother fed many who were hungry and she'd have plates delivered to folks throughout the neighborhood. I always knew she was active in her church, but I didn't know she was the president of a number of auxiliaries and she was a well-respected member of the community. Beyond that, she'd also spearheaded the neighborhood lunch program. She was responsible for the lunch truck that delivered food daily to the kids in the neighborhood. Now I understood why it was so important to her that we took advantage of the service.

Tammi, drenched in tears, stood up and gave a speech thanking everyone for their cards and expressions of sympathy. For the first time in my life, I actually empathized with her. Unlike me, she didn't grow up with her father and she even lived away from her mother at times. For the first few years of her life, she lived with Grandma. That's why she was the only grandchild to refer to her as "Mama." To her, our grandmother was more like her mother and our aunts and uncles were like the sisters and brothers she never had. I guess I understood why they coddled her. Perhaps Grandma sensed that she filled a void in Tammi's life and that's why she allowed Tammi to serve as her fourteenth child. I don't know if I was actually on to something, but it really didn't matter at that point. What mattered was that an era in my life was ending and there wasn't a damn thing I could do about it.

Suddenly, I appreciated those summer days that had seemed almost unbearable during my childhood. Keeping house would have been a good habit to acquire. In fact, I wish I'd paid more attention when Grandma canned preserves, made jelly, quilted, and did all of those other special things that had been passed down from her own grandmother. At first, I thought Grandma didn't cherish her grandchildren the way other grandmothers did, but at that moment I knew she loved us so much she was willing to invest in us. I realized that loving family isn't always about giving what's wanted, but mostly it's giving what's needed.

And what I needed right then was to turn back the hands of time so I could tell my grandmother that I finally understood. But it was too late for me. I could only hope that as I entered womanhood I would take the few things that I did learn with me and pass them on to my own children.

Rule number six: cherish the time you have with your family while you still have the time to let them know how much you appreciate them.

Take heed of the wisdom of our elders, because they've already seen what we have yet to see. What lessons of faith and spirituality are you prepared to teach our next generations?

# *O My Divine*

## By Emily Diane Gunter

*O my divine Heavenly Mother,*
*The will and wisdom of God,*
*Come to me now in this open space*
*For this new day,*
*Fresh and unused.*
*Mother, show me the blueprint for*
*My life today.*
*O my Divine Heavenly Father,*
*Come to me now,*
*And fill this new space*
*With your beautiful loving light*
*And consciousness.*

# Journey To Peace And Serenity

# Miss Grace Is in the House

## By Maria Denise Dowd

How do we get around the rolling bends and valleys of past broods, future worries, and present mind trips? How do we tame the thoughts that wallow, race, and then wallow around in our minds? How do we unplug the fatty, overloaded circuits of our consciousness? How do we go about sorting out our humanness when it's been meshed and melded into the strident ways of Westerners? Is it truly possible to empower ourselves to move into quiet enlightenment?

I'm not going to pretend to have answers to these questions. I've walked the hypocritical line far too often to fake my way to a deep, thoughtful reply. What I *think* I know is that too many of us subconsciously put a stranglehold on our—and often others'—need for peace and serenity.

We wrestle with our habits of squeezing too much into too little time. Consequently, we find ourselves too exhausted to enjoy peace and serenity. Or, we waste time listening to or living out loud the *woe are mes*, then find ourselves tossing and turning those little bits of peace and serenity into unrecognizable globs of noisy, self-discontent.

Instead of embracing mind-quieting practices, we busy ourselves squashed behind the steering wheels of rescues, displaced obligations, and frustrating attempts to do it all ourselves. Whatever happened to the concept of carpooling or taking the more scenic route... then stopping to smell the roses? How do we go about shutting out the synthetic clamors of day-to-day living to relish those sounds that please the soul?

Our challenge is to check our self-proclaimed superwoman, Miss Martyr in all her weighty glory, at the door. Our challenge is not to let Miss Martyr park her portly butt in the best room *with a view*—in our house of solace. We invite her in, and she invariably overstays her welcome. And, boy, does Miss Martyr love to eat away at our souls, leaving crumbs and spills all over the place!

Missy takes her fleshy fingers and dishevels our spirit, then entangles them in our misbelief that we have to keep doing, and doing frenetically, to get to that "higher" place. We'd rather allow our minds, bodies, and spirits to be taken over by what we should and must do, giving Miss Martyr permission to lash out. And she does so boisterously, just to hear her own loud mouth. We engage her in raucous, meddlesome conversations of doom and gloom and forget to set the clock for tranquility-enhancing rites and rituals. Trying to play host to Miss Martyr can take its toll.

Have teatime, but don't invite *her* into our private parlors. With feet up, let's pour ourselves cups of stillness and stir heaping spoonfuls of serenity into our hearts. When we quiet ourselves and experience conscious breath, if only for fifteen to thirty minutes each day, we will begin to see the light . . . and experience things lighter. Deep breathing, meditation, a walk outdoors, a stretch out on the couch, an aromatic bath, a massage, or yoga is on the short list. You might add gardening, spiritual reading, journaling, or chanting to yours. I know that my favorite sound is no sound. *That* I know. Rest assured when our souls open up, Miss Grace, and maybe even Miss Ease, will step in and serve Miss Martyr her eviction notice.

By incorporating rituals and arrangements that bring "ahhhhh" quietude into our lives, we'll discover the magic of personal renewal, a heightened sense of intimacy, and a love for self so spectacular, you'll rarely (I'll never say never) be inclined to let the heaviness of Miss Martyr back in.

So, tune out the distractions and tune into your inner self and nature. God didn't put all of this beauty around us as an exercise in futility. Turn your television off and turn your inner vision on. And have an ease- and grace-filled journey to peace and serenity.

*Journey to Peace and Serenity*

I empower myself to allow more ease and grace into my life today. By acknowledging those things that are uncomforting in my life, I release their hold on my spirit. Today, I will let go of . . .

# *Unearthed*

## By Gequeta Valentine

*I was well into my early thirties when I realized*
*That I was living my life with my head and not my heart.*
*No matter how hard I try, I still can't remember the exact moment*
*When I decided to ignore my thriving spirit to accommodate the world*
*And its weighty expectations of me.*
*My blind eye would subsequently result in the splintering of my soul*
*And soon thereafter my identity, as I subtly adjusted,*
*Compressing my individuality into the neatly drawn box that society had so*
*Self-righteously constructed for me.*
*Consumed by an existence without substance,*
*I pressed on, eagerly pursuing that which I'd been bred to regard as essential.*

*Status, wealth, power, and prestige!*
*The world's golden stamp of approval.*

*And so I sought after such things, vigorously pursuing them,*
*One after the other, until my desires were fulfilled,*
*But even then I remained in a constant state of yearning.*
*I wanted to be more, do more, and have more,*
*Never fully understanding that what I really needed was to love more.*

*Myself.*

*To dizzying heights and beyond, love my uniqueness, my brilliant, rhythmic, splendid*
*Nature, which the world had no hand in creating.*
*Why now do I wonder, did I ever feel the need to look outside of myself*
*For validation and approval when my own acceptance of me was more than enough? But would it be enough to get me back to that peaceful, purposeful place*
*Where I knew I needed to be, that place that existed solely inside me, untouched,*
*Untainted, in its purest form?*

*With boldness I stepped forward and began to purge, determined to undo that which*
*Had been done in the name of integration, to unearth that which had taken years of*
*Obsession and suppression, to bury, to rid myself of the need to look like, sound like,*
*And be like.*
*Somewhere underneath it all dwelled my raw identity and I longed to release her.*
*To once and for all live without asking the world's permission.*

*Slowly, painfully I pared away the layers of my foreign interior,*
*In search of what I desperately needed to still be there.*
*Through tears and self-doubt, I prayed, waited, and listened, hoping to hear, see, or feel*
*Some semblance of a being that I could recognize as my own.*
*And when I, suspended in between, could wait no longer, she emerged.*
*More exuberant and explosive than even I could ever have imagined.*
*And I saw her and knew her. For she was I and I she, and I loved her, more deeply,*
*More intimately, more passionately than I'd ever dared before.*

Journey to Peace and Serenity

*She is strong, honest, thoughtful, confident, outspoken, courageous, endearing,*
*Courteous, graceful, zealous, humble, yielding, modest, joyful, gracious, and carefree.*

*She is all these things and more. But most of all . . . she is me.*

A picture is worth a thousand words. Create a portrait of you in your most peaceful and serene state of being. What thoughts are on your mind? Describe you in your most meditative of states and how you feel. . . .

*Journey to Peace and Serenity*

# *Rearview Mirror*

## By Maria Denise Dowd

My God, how we beat the hell out of our own selves, fists balled, battering our psyches to a bloody pulp. What is it about us womenfolk? We work far too hard on *not* liking ourselves. We overdo and overkill, then are ready to kill again over the most trite things—our weight, our complexion, our hair, our jobs, our men, our cash. Did I mention our weight, our hair, and our men?

I'm calling for all of us womenfolk to give it a rest, already. Me too. I have no solid reason to exclude my own self from this tongue-lashing. I'm guilty as charged: 8:04 a.m. . . . sneaked a peek at my forty-plus-inch hips, hopeful that this time *they*, excuse me, *it* looked a bit more like somebody else's. 10:36 a.m. . . . thought about putting on my "face," even though my man repeatedly tells me I look more radiant without it. The cosmetic industry doesn't believe him, so why should I? 12:47 p.m. . . . regretted not going to my yoga or kickboxing class that started exactly thirty-four minutes *before* that wishful glance at my rear end for the umpteenth time this week.

Why do we burn ourselves so, and then scorch others along the way? Why can we not smile at our reflection in the mirror and in another woman's face? Why do we fry, lye, dye, and lie ourselves into this tightly wound mass of torment, then proceed to smash things up around us—feelings, egos, friendships, and love relationships . . . not to mention our own tender spirits? Why do we care so dang much about those things that matter the least and get amnesia over the things that count? How often do we, after the fact, look over our shoulder and ask, "Oh, was that me who forgot to exercise today?" "Oh, was that me who forgot to give thanks last night?" "Oh, shoot, didn't I promise myself that I'd stop trippin' over that situation that I have absolutely no control over?"

My daughter has said repeatedly that girls her age have lost their minds, quick to pick a fight with a girl over a boy who may not even have developed the capacity to respect the girl's body or mind, much less her divinity. As mothers, we shake our heads and heed warnings about staying away from "those crazy girls," yet deny that we've lost our own minds, quick to pick a fight with ourselves because we may not even have developed the capacity to respect our own bodies, minds, and divinity . . . then we pass this madness on to our daughters. Instead of wanting a piece of her over there, we should seek out some peace of mind right here.

We've got to stop looking at our rearview mirrors and start loving the vision before us. We've got to stop looking into those distorting images, slyly stylized by the Monopoly Man with dollar signs for eyeballs and heart. Let's stop trying to fit our very round pegs into that very square hole, relentlessly forcing our nature into a space that doesn't compute with our reality . . . not remotely.

So, let's be real and true to ourselves.

Let's be true to ourselves and true to our spirit. Let's look into that mirror and *love* the woman we see . . . wholly.

Let's be true to ourselves and true to our Village. Let's look into her eyes and his . . . and love the person we see . . . wholly.

Self-acceptance and love are the ability to see light when looking inward. Here are the qualities that I illuminate . . .

# *No More*

## By Shellie Warren

No more waking up in the morning with my first priority not being prayer.
No more setting the clock a half hour early to paint on features that ain't even there.
No more skipping breakfast and picking up a biscuit on the way to work.
I could warm up a bagel while warming up my car,
Instead of wondering why it's running funny.
No more walking into the office with a nasty attitude,
Reminiscing over what happened the day before.
No more clocking in late, then demanding more hours,
Getting denied, then wondering why I'm poor.
No more lunches of French fries instead of a salad, Coke instead of water, candy
Instead of fruit.
No more complaining afterward why I'm edgy, my face is splotchy, that my waistline's pudgy.

*No more getting off work and hitting up the cell on my ride home.*
*The messages can wait and the solitude would do me good.*
*No more going off in traffic jams, it's five o'clock and I need to chill.*
*No more stopping by the convenience store for chips and a magazine.*
*No more consulting fashion magazines without consulting my conscience.*
*No more succumbing to the media's definition of the twenty-five Sexiest.*
*No more comparing my relationship, wealth, or emotional stability*
*To the hottest couple on the latest magazine cover.*
*No more depending on cosmetic or hair-care companies to define my beauty.*
*No more envying the other girls' long tresses or skintight dresses.*
*True beauty cannot be bought in weaves, perms, or push-up bras.*
*No more apologetic explanations for my natural crop, vintage style, full-lipped,*
*Overbitten smile.*
*No more letting someone else's insecurities intimidate me.*
*No more suppressing my feelings for fear of your offense.*
*No more coming home to a messy house, unwashed clothes, and unpaid bills.*

*No more going straight to the idiot box or CD player without thanking God for*
*Another day.*
*No more consulting "the soaps" before scripture.*
*No more hurried showers in the evening, I deserve a bubble bath.*
*No more broken nails, chipped toe polish, or ashy skin.*
*Or missed repetitions of "I'm Every Woman," "There's no one like me," and "I have a prepared destiny."*
*No more worrying about who said what, who went where, or if I should be there.*
*No more giving when I don't want to.*
*No more second-guessing answers to questions already given by God.*
*No more going into relationships, unprepared and unaware.*
*No more depressing love songs of prolonged relationships gone wrong.*
*No more being the ex-girlfriend martyr, the codependent counselor, or the jealous*
*Friend.*
*No more regurgitation of the pain someone has caused.*
*No more holding grudges against those who have transgressed.*
*No more being the manic, the workaholic, the sex-addicted, the suppressed gifted, the*
*Disrespected, the doormat, or the openly rejected.*

*No more failing already-taken tests.*
*No more waiting for my ship to come in.*
*No more not learning how to swim.*
*No more lying to myself or withholding the truth.*
*No more hurting deep down and healing up in the mall.*
*No more entertaining your mess or creating my own.*
*No more holding on to what ain't mine.*
*No more crying to God about consequences I've suffered.*
*No more doubting after I've prayed.*
*No more idolizing the companionship of a man or children.*
*No more being ungrateful for the times when you've tolerated my shortcomings,*
*Mistakes, aches, and pains.*
*No more consciously repeating them again, and again, and again.*
*No more riding the line of Christian love and self-abuse.*
*No more expecting the same of you.*
*No more giving God less than what he created.*
*No more cursing past soul ties, mental fears, or unanswered prayers.*
*I'm his creature, God said it, I believe it, and that settles it.*
*No more delaying what's mine.*
*No more wanting what I'm not willing to give.*
*No more settling for the consciously negative.*
*No more merely existing, I'm ready to live!*

*No more helping a man cheat because of . . . or on me.*
*No more being a hypocrite to the teenage girl or entertaining the hormonal boy.*
*No more first expecting that Mr. Right should be fine.*
*No more sitting on the couch versus sit-ups on the floor.*
*No more buying a new dress before giving to the poor.*
*No more accepting the reputation of being "loose."*
*No more giving my all without expecting so much more.*
*No more scratching the surface without touching the core.*
*It's a new day and I know what I want.*
*It's God's best.*
*No more settling for less.*
*No more.*
*No more.*
*No more.*

Proclaim yours! Declare your "no mores" with commitment and jubilation. Celebrate your release of things that mess with your peace and serenity. . . .

*Journey to Peace and Serenity*

# *The Peace Process*

## By Debrena Jackson Gandy

Peace, peace, peace. In this postmodern, high-tech, fast-paced, instant culture in which we live, there seems to be something that we sistahs are seeking but aren't finding. There seems to be something we've become obsessed with—finding peace and serenity. Why all the hype about peace? What's the big deal about serenity? I think because both are dangerously absent in our lives.

When you are at peace, there is all absence of conflict, tension, and hostility within you. When you are at peace, you are free from internal disturbance and restlessness—conditions that can result from worrying too much, trying to micromanage and overcontrol relationships in your life, feeling guilty or fearful, angry, scattered, resentful, disappointed, or jealous. Serenity is the result of being calm; it is also about being clear.

When peace is missing in your life, you become dangerous to yourself and to others. You become dangerous because a mind, body, and spirit without peace equal a restless mind, a tension-filled body, and a depleted spirit. When peace and serenity are missing in your life, you become dangerous because you are used to being in a state of conflict and stress, and when it is absent, even for a short time, you get to creating drama and stirrin' up mess so that you can be in your comfort zone again, so that you can be back to what is familiar to you. And when we don't have inner peace and serenity in our lives, we become susceptible to different forms of addiction as a way to escape our discomfort, temporarily distract us, or give us what seems to be a short-term pain fix.

Yes, there are socially sanctioned and acceptable activity-based addictions, such as shopping too much, and working too much. Then there are the addictions that society has deemed unacceptable and immoral, such as being addicted to drugs or alcohol. Both types of addictions are a result of inner emptiness and unhealed emotional and spiritual wounds. But don't be fooled. We also have the more insidious addictions, such as lying, pretending we are something we are not, and gossiping.

So how do we find peace? Yes, peace is something we want, something we know is important to our well-being, but we don't always know how to make it real in our lives. Where do we begin? We begin by doing some spiritual housecleaning. Contrary to popular belief, being at peace is not just a matter of learning to meditate or pray more. To be at peace requires that we also handle unfinished business, clean up incomplete, festering issues, and clear the three Cs out of our lives: clutter, chaos, and confusion.

*Journey to Peace and Serenity*

This clearing out may mean releasing leftover bad feelings from a past relationship with a sisterfriend, parent, or boyfriend. Do you need to have a conversation that will allow you to communicate from your heart? Do you need to write a letter that expresses your interpretation of a situation that occurred and what you feel is the resolution? Do you need to begin an exercise program that will enable you to release anger and frustration from your body? Whom do you need to forgive? It just might be yourself. Are you harboring guilt, regret, disappointment, or resentment from your past? You can't hold on to guilt, regrets, resentment, frustration, and disappointments and be at peace. These are mutually exclusive. Serenity will constantly elude you.

Being at peace means removing the toxic emotional clutter that has accumulated in your current relationship. Not only is there emotional clutter that we need to spring-clean from our lives, there is also physical clutter. You know what I'm talking about—piles of paper, stacks of old bills, stale food in the refrigerator, junk in your car trunk, clothes that you haven't worn in years hanging in your closet, receipts and crumpled dollar bills stuffed in your wallet, a cluttered purse or makeup bag, dirty clothes overflowing from the hamper, French fries and candy wrappers under your car seat. Can I get a witness? And, sistah, I can definitely relate. Spring-cleaning is an ongoing process, not just one that happens in the spring. And to be at peace, it is necessary.

*Journey to a Blissful Life*

Quiet time is also an important ingredient of peacefulness. Our lives are filled with constant activity, noise, and rippin' and runnin'. Quiet time is about integrating blocks of time into your life that are free of noise and frenetic activity. This may include praying, meditating, writing, journaling, drawing, quilting, bathing, taking a walk, or sitting quietly and reflecting, to name a few things. Quiet time allows your spirit to recover from the attacks that are made on it in the course of your daily life. Quiet time allows your spirit to take a breather and rejuvenate itself. Without quiet time, our spiritual gas tanks are constantly on E. Quiet time is a way to refuel your spirit.

Peace is experienced, not found or achieved. And it is experienced as we replace the crisis, chaos, clutter, and confusion in our lives with calm and clarity. The belief that life has to be hard and a struggle keep us in perpetual cycles of tension and stress. This does not have to be. You have the ability to change and transform your reality from one of stress and internal restlessness, to one of peace. Take it one step at a time, and remember to be patient with yourself. Experiencing peace is a process, not an event.

Today, my heart sings with peace of mind, body, and soul. Here are the small steps I pledge to take to bring about greater peace and ease in my life. I acknowledge that I don't have to do them all right now, but quietly will clear a path for my wisdom to guide me. . . .

# A Matter of Taste

## By Mary Elizabeth Paschall

*Once it was hard*
*To say* Thank God
*For friendships gone awry,*

*I'd feel rejected,*
*Blame myself,*
*Sometimes I'd even cry,*

*Now I know that*
*Time spent with friends,*
*Once shared is never wasted,*

*So I give thanks*
*For sweet laughter*
*and salty tears*
*I've tasted.*

## *Love Thy Neighbor*

### By Nicole Gailliard

*Peace I leave with you; my peace I give you. I do not give to you as the world gives. Do not let your hearts be troubled and do not be afraid.*
—John 14:27 [New International Version]

About four years ago, my family and I lived in a neighborhood that was anything but sprawling. If someone was playing blackjack next door, I could tell you the next card to be thrown. There was a young man who lived directly behind us who loved to entertain us with his music. Unfortunately for me, his taste in music clashed with mine. This fact did not seem to bother him or lessen his intent to bless me with his flavor of tunes. His music arrived at inopportune times, and at decibels even the astronauts would frown upon hearing. The language in the music was offensive at best, insulting and humiliating more routinely. The angrier I got, the louder and more vulgar the music seemed to become.

I felt the need for a change. After all, this situation was ruining my peace and causing constant frustration. I was beginning to feel animosity not only toward the gentleman playing the music, but everyone in his home and the rest of my neighbors as well. Why did his music seemingly bother only me? I began to pray on it. I prayed not only that the music would stop, but also that the gentlemen would have a change of heart. I prayed that whatever was going on in his life that made him relish the language, the stories, and the characters found in the chorus of his music would somehow be cleaned away from his life. Why was this type of "music" so attractive to him? Why was this type of music allowed in his home?

God is so incredibly awesome in his plans, including the part about us loving our neighbor. In other words, I have to love you enough to pray for you, in order for justice to be served. God does not allow us to be selfish, prideful, or boastful, or to seek revenge. He has taught me that when I let go and allow him to have his way, he will take care of people who have caused discomfort in our lives.

Well, back to the story.

The music stopped; or had it?

Then, it dawned me on.

The music was still playing. The change had taken place in *me*.

Suddenly, I didn't hear the language anymore. Suddenly, I was not offended by the characterization of women in the music. Suddenly, I was at peace with my neighbor . . . *after* I had decided to act in love.

*Journey to Peace and Serenity*

Finally, the Bible tells us that we should think on things that are true and noble, and pure and lovely, and that if we do this, the peace of God will be with us.

And that, my neighbor, my friend . . . is my story.

I acknowledge that I've held on to past transgressions "done" to me by someone who was once close to my heart. It's time for me to take ownership of my pain, detachment, or grief. Today, I make the following amends with myself to begin healing this wound on my soul. By doing so, I will be more whole and ready to receive and bestow compassion, love, and respect. . . .

# *Love Affair*

## By Kimberly T. Matthews

May I share a secret with you? I'm only telling you because you seem trustworthy enough. I am involved in a very deep and serious love affair. This affair started so subtly, as most of them do. This "relationship," if you will, crept up on me without my even noticing or purposing in my heart to be committed to such a thing. I didn't mean to become so fiercely and passionately entangled, and now that I've turned my head to look back over my shoulder at the path that this relationship has traveled, I'm fascinated that I've been involved for more than eight years! Eight years! My, how one day rolls into the next!

As with any relationship, I've experienced the typical ups and downs, but I've embraced and endured every storm, no matter how upsetting. There have been mornings when I've awakened and asked myself what was going on. Nevertheless, as I pondered the journey, I knew I wouldn't end it. There have been evenings when I just didn't feel like dealing with the drama of this union any longer, yet I pressed on. And what would any union be if there weren't a few nights of going to bed angry and teary-eyed, not knowing if the bond would last beyond the wee hours of the morning? Then, of course, there is always a makeup period that overpowers any dispute to the point where I can't even remember what the conflict was about in the first place.

As tempted as I have sometimes been to end it all, I just refuse to let it go. Just when I've thought that I couldn't take it anymore, something happens to make me smile, laugh, and feel simply wonderful about this love I'm experiencing. Something always draws me back, calming my emotions from the greatest peak of frustration, and settles in the center of my heart. Even when I want to stay upset, I find that I can't. Rather than my saying, "It's over," the words "I love you" tumble across my lips. Rather than packing up and throwing out every single item that brings the slightest notion of this union to my mind, before I build up enough nerve and true sincerity to do so, I find myself coaxing on this intimacy.

A few friends have offered their personal opinions about this whole thing, giving me thoughtless recommendations, suggesting what they would do, and even going as far as to communicate what their individual visions are for me! What nerve! They say things like, "Chile, you good, because if it was me, then this and that!" I listen sometimes . . . just to humor them; sometimes I don't. Some are even silly enough to think that I'm trapped in this thing. "You ain't got to do that," they say. They think that I believe that there are no other options out there for me. Oh, how wrong they are. On the contrary, this is an affair of my choosing! I don't express this to them, but on the inside I stand up defiantly and say, "I'm grown. I can have an affair if I want to." Forgive me if I seem defensive, but this is true love, y'all. They don't understand, but that's okay, because this love is all about me. It's who I am, what I want, and what I like. So talk about me all you want; I'm keeping on anyway.

As Usher would say, I got it bad. And I'm lovin' every minute of this affair . . . with my natural hair.

# *Maturity*

## By Reverend Victoria Lee-Owens

*Maturity ain't so bad*
*No...*
*Growing up really isn't all that difficult*
*If after a while you learn the subtle difference*
*between holding hands and being held hostage*

*You learn that love doesn't mean being locked down*
*Or being totally dependent upon one another*
*By facing your fears...*
*You find that company doesn't mean staying just for security*

*You start to see that a kiss isn't an act of commitment*
*Ain't no promise given with most presents...*
*And "I want you" doesn't always mean "until the end of time"*

*Moving toward a peace-filled place called serenity*
*You begin to tolerate your shortcomings*

*Facing errors made with head held high*
*Knowing that amends means trying not to ever do that again*
*Rather than apologizing over and over about the same thing*

*Your eyes look straight ahead in a confident stance*
*As you trade the uncertainties of a little girl for the grace of a woman*
*Affirming that love is much stronger than one's ego*
*And pride can be overcome by creating bridges of understanding*

*You learn to build avenues in the span of a day*
*Because tomorrow's ground is too uncertain*
*And you learn to stop making New Year's resolutions*
*Since it seems they get lost before the next week*
*Instead you wake up each day affirming self*
*Though all around seems bleak and barren*

*You timidly begin tending your own garden of wisdom*
*Noting what seeds season your life*
*And after a while you realize*
*That holding on to something serving no useful purpose*
*Will leave a coldness in your heart . . .*
*Just like the iciness of wintertime*
*If you linger unprotected in it too long*

*You compliment yourself and find it's really okay . . .*
*As much as if not more . . .*
*Than waiting for a rush of good feelings*
*Occasionally brought by the words of others*
*Sure . . . you can gracefully embrace that as well*

*You stop waiting for somebody else*
*To bring you flowers and jewels and perfume*
*You know exactly what you like*
*And if unsure you use the power of choice . . .*
*One or many*

*You learn that you really do count for more . . .*
*You're not a toy or shiny "for display only" object*
*You are somebody . . .*
*Smart and strong and enduring and loving and gracious*
*Really quite charming*

*And with every hello and good-bye said on passing days*
*You learn another lesson*
*You are a wise woman*
*A grand dame*
*Divinely spirit aware*
*Soulful*

*Dignified*
*Regal*
*And of course most beautiful . . .*
*In maturity*

# Our Quest for Peace

## By Maria Denise Dowd and Jewel Diamond Taylor

### Our Bodies, Our Temples

Jewel: At night, your body is preparing for rest and a fast. Visualize your resting organs trying to push through heavy foods. Not a pleasant sight. Eat more lightly to sleep more tightly.

Maria: I drink water constantly and usually keep glasses all over the house—on my nightstand, on the kitchen counter, near my computer, in the living room, and in the bathroom. I drink from these glasses all day and all night.

### In the Bedroom

Maria: Tornado-torn bedrooms are suffocating. Rarely does an item of clothing stay off of a hanger or out of a drawer for longer than a day or two. I never watch television or bring work into my bedroom. My bed gets made every day. The idea of tumbling into an already tumbled bed gives me goose bumps.

Jewel: Clean up the clutter and maintain your bedroom as a place of peace, love, serenity, and refuge. Don't watch TV violence and news, pay your bills, or argue in your bedroom. The negative energy of stress and mess will linger there and affect your consciousness, the quality of intimacy with your mate, and the quality of your sleep.

Maria: I once bought a comforter based purely on its cheap price. It was hard, lackluster, and smelled like turpentine. I stuffed it back into the plastic zippered bag and circled back to the store to return it. Instead, I invested in the one I fell in love with at *first sight*. Its swirling pattern reminds me of gusty Caribbean seas. Each night I *submerge* myself. Don't let practicality override your joy.

Jewel: Don't cheat yourself; treat yourself to quality pillows, linen, and a comfortable mattress, proper ventilation, soothing colors on the wall, living plants, and pleasant aromas.

### On Relaxation and Meditation

Jewel: I treated myself to one of those small indoor waterfalls because the sound of water is so soothing. When I rise in the morning I have my morning prayer and meditation standing in my front window gazing out at a beautiful park as I look upon the pictures by the window of my parents and other relatives who have passed on. Also on this altar are pictures of my family and friends who are living. I begin my day thanking God for my health and for waking up to see a new day. I bless and pray for my family in this world and those in eternal sleep. This spiritual exercise helps me to focus on my priorities, serenity and gratitude.

Maria: I love absolute quiet. Televisions and high-tempo music overload my already hyper mind. I thank God for tranquility and for the capacity to hear the birdsong and the rhythm of my own breath. From my favorite resting place—my couch—I never tire of imagining the artists, whose works adorn much of my wall space, exquisitely translating their feelings and stories into color, shape, and texture.

Jewel: I agree with the advice about living with peace from Katherine Dunham: "Go within every day and find the inner strength so that the world will not blow your candle out." I do that each day by stepping away from the demands of the day to pause for the cause. I screen my calls, take my shoes off, drink a glass of water, review my priorities for the day to avoid any frantic running around, call and connect with a family member or friend to take my mind off of work or worry and to laugh or share some love and encouragement with. I also listen to my music or write in my journal or just give myself permission to sit awhile and do nothing.

Maria: I treat myself to *two-hour* massages in my home. My therapist has added hot stones into the mix. Ahhhhhhh. Regularly? I'm working on it.

## On Exercise

Jewel: For my physical exercise, I alternate between brisk walking outside in early morning while listening to gospel music, or I practice yoga or do aerobics with soul videos and exercise with them.

Maria: For aerobics, I love and teach an Afro-Latin Groove class at a local fitness club. I enjoy yoga. I'm *trying* to incorporate spinning into my mix. I go reggae dancing almost every weekend. And I'm into weight training . . . very good for forty-plus women.

## On Crazy-makers, Drama Queens, and Kings, Too

Jewel and Maria: It's important to recognize and stay away from the crazy-makers, drama queens, and energy vampires in your life.

Discern and put space between you and those who are prone to dole out jabs and needle pricks. They drain energy, faith, and enthusiasm right out of you.

## Bathing Rituals

Jewel: I'm a morning person. I enjoy a soothing bath with Epsom salts and a combination of eucalyptus and peppermint oils. The deep-breathing exercises and the hot steam help to loosen the joints, and breathing the stimulating aromas in my bath brings energy and clear thinking.

Maria: I rarely go to sleep without taking my nightly warm soak in a bubbly bath. I often exfoliate with a Warm Spirit body polish. I read, perspire, and before long I'm drifting. I massage my skin head to toe with a shea-butter and olive-oil-rich body butter and crawl immediately into bed. I'm a very early riser, so I never have any problems falling right off to sleep.

## On Clutter

Maria: Clutter doesn't stand a chance in my life. I'm more focused and productive and have greater peace of mind when my surroundings are in order. I once read in an "organize-your-life" book, "When you don't have time for the bowling balls, handle the marbles." Dumping junk drawer contents into a trash bag and walking it outdoors really takes only minutes. My junk mail never hits anything but the trash can. Because I work from home, I often have my house professionally cleaned a day or two before I leave town. It's satisfying to know that I'm going to return to a clean house, as it takes three to four days to catch my breath and follow up on phone calls, e-mail, and snail mail. I know that I don't handle thoughts of housework very well, so I diffuse them by being proactive.

Jewel: I'm learning more and more to get rid of clutter in my house and the clutter in my life. Letting go of old stuff and old thinking produces more room for God to show up in my life. It is an act of faith to let go of something because I'm trusting and knowing that it will be replaced with something better. To renew ourselves, we must learn to release. Release the old breath and breathe in new breath. Release worry and receive peace. Release the old newspapers and old junk collecting dust. When your home and your mind are free of junk and clutter, you will feel more peaceful.

Maria: When the clutter or house maintenance load is too much to handle yourself, hire someone to do it for you. It may not be an issue of not being able to afford it, but simply a budgetary trade-off. Ask yourself, "What do I need to *trade up* to have greater peace and serenity in my life?" The answer is usually quite apparent; you simply need to acknowledge that truth and act upon it.

Rituals are detailed methods of procedure faithfully or regularly followed. The role that rituals can play in my life is far-reaching and will go a long way to adding greater fulfillment, joy, relationship-building, and intimacy for me and mine.

Describe a ritual or two you will incorporate into your life and what added value it will bring to the quality of your life. . . .

# Serenity Prayer: 23rd Psalm for Busy People

## By Jewel Diamond Taylor

The Lord is my pace-setter, I shall not rush.

As I let go of the hurry and worry, I am comforted with God's blessed assurance that all is in divine order. So I breathe, relax, and rest my mind and body.

God provides me with refuges of peace and order to restore my sanity and soul. He leads me in what to do, what to delegate, and what to dump to create calmness in my mind.

Even though I have a great many things to accomplish today, I will not fret or stress, for his presence and power are here within. I will not sweat the small stuff.

Every day I am led and fed by the Holy Spirit. His will and purpose for my life keep me clear, not confused, blessed, not stressed.

He prepares refreshments and renewal in the midst of my activities by anointing my head with his oil of tranquility.

My cup of gratitude and joy overflows. Surely, surely harmony, success, and prosperity shall be the fruit of my labor, for I shall walk in the promise and peace of the Lord and dwell in his house of love, protection, provision, health, and wealth forever.

Today, I will strive for clarity in my life. I will focus and breathe a mere sixty seconds of my energy on that one thing that is creating clutter and blockage. Here's what that one thing is and how I'll celebrate my forward movement after I've completed this task . . .

## *The Wind of Change*

### By Stephanie J. Gates

For two years it rained in my life almost daily. The thunderstorms, downpours, and even light drizzles soaked my spirit. Misery and despair seeped into my being as the "wind of change" blew into my life and wreaked havoc in one form or another—a new job, a new residence, a dissolved relationship, and a series of other mishaps that blocked the sun from shining in my life. Surrounded by people who loved me and having a job at times when many people were out of work, I was beating myself up because I didn't think I had a "right" to be sad. Yet the tears continued to fall as the rain beat against my soul.

On an emotional roller coaster, I just could not get myself together. Dying was out of the question, but so was living. I was just existing, and that was painful for me because I loved life. One day, at the health club, I struck up a conversation with a woman who was a member of Team Dream, a woman-of-color triathlon training team, and she invited me to a meeting. Listening to her and feeling her energy, I decided that it wouldn't hurt to check it out. I had nothing to lose.

I was awed. Not only was each woman on a personal journey to "raise her game," the Team Dream motto, but each was also there to be of service to her fellow teammates and to her community. Positive energy lit up the room, and that was something I wanted and needed. I had talked three of my friends into going with me, but they decided not to join. However, I signed up and talked my sister-in-law into joining, too. Maybe change was not the unwelcome guest I thought it to be. Being the nonathlete who ran from gym class, I was actually considering participation in a sport that I erroneously believed was for white men only.

I was quiet and observant in the beginning. It was as if I'd walked into a dreamworld, and if I got too excited, I'd wake up and discover it wasn't real. Everything I needed as an athlete, a teammate, and a friend, I received from Team Dream. I couldn't sing the praises of Team Dream loud enough to anyone who would listen. I looked forward to biking on Monday, swimming on Wednesday, and circuit training on Saturday, and anything else that would "put me in the game."

Of course, there were many days when I was bothered, tired, agitated, or a combination of all three, but I trained anyway, because I knew that my teammates would be holding umbrellas of smiles, laughter, encouragement, and support. Slowly, the cloud hanging over my life lifted. The sun started peeking through, and it would show itself for the rest the day. Being a part of Team Dream enabled me to embrace the changes that were taking place in my life. Things were better, though every now and then, I felt the rain dripping into my thoughts.

The closer we got to my first triathlon of the season, the more I began to doubt myself. There were times when the thought of participating overwhelmed me, and I wanted to pull out until the following year. I was particularly afraid of the open-water swim. But I refused to stop working at it, and I knew that if I got over the mental hurdles I'd be okay. Surrounded by nothing but the best from my teammates and coaches, as well as the support from family and friends, I knew that the only thing standing in my way was me. So, taking one of my teammate's advice, I got out of my own way. I kept training with the end in mind. I saw myself talking to new dreamers *after* I had completed a triathlon. And when I stopped fighting myself, it happened. I completed two triathlons during the summer of 2004, and I look forward to sharing my story with new teammates who will wonder what they got themselves into. And I'll tell them—one of the best experiences in their lives.

I *love* Team Dream! And this is one dream I hope I don't have to wake from any time soon.

There's nothing like a dream team or "purpose posse" (read *Journey to Empowerment*) to shake up the soul and get the blood pumping. Here is a list of my awesome dream team I'm grateful for . . . and, after I'm done here, I'll write each of them a note to let them know . . .

# Basking in the Beauty of Life

## By Valorie Burton

In the midst of our hectic schedules, truly noticing nature forces us to be present in the moment. Nature moves at its own pace—unconcerned with the frantic pace of the human world and unaffected by whether or not we choose to acknowledge its presence. Nature is always there—living, splendid, and offering to be noticed.

Special moments are around us every day. Some are more breathtaking than others, but the moments are there if we will open our lives to experiencing them. Often, those who have the most obvious opportunities to bask in the beauty of nature are least likely to do so. It was not until I moved to a place less blessed with the natural beauty than the places I had previously lived that I finally recognized my numerous missed opportunities. From birth until I moved to Dallas in 1994, I had always lived in some of the most awe-inspiring places in the world. When I was a wide-eyed little girl living at Tyndall Air Force Base in my birthplace of Panama City, Florida, my backyard faced the Gulf of Mexico. The water washed ashore just one hundred feet from the edge of our backyard. I would swing and look at the ocean. I recall often sitting on my father's shoulders in our living room and peering through binoculars to watch the dolphins playfully jump around the poles that stood a few yards out from the shore. I was just five or six years old and I thought that everyone had dolphins in their backyard. Thirteen years later, when I began attending Florida State University, I took the beach for granted, visiting the beach only once during my college career!

After I arrived in the vibrant but landlocked and mountainless city of Dallas, I yearned for the opportunity to drive to the beach or the mountains in less than an hour. After my having lived near the beautiful white-sand, emerald coast of Florida; the wine-producing mountains, winding rivers, and grand castles of Germany; the magnificent Rockies of Colorado; and the dramatic cliffs and picturesque views of Monterey, California, it seemed almost ironic that I could appreciate the simple beauty of the trees, parks, and man-made lakes of Dallas, Texas. But I appreciated them very much. I looked forward to my walks to the neighborhood park. There, I would sit on one of the large boulders that line the park's trail, breathe deeply, and absorb the beauty of the sights and sounds around me—the blue sky, the bright flowers, or even the energetic giggle of a child playing in the park. Whatever was the vibe of the day, I absorbed.

It brings joy to our days when we bask in the beauty of life. We must learn to deliberately engage ourselves in these kinds of moments by shifting our lives out of overdrive. When you are in overdrive, your mind and body are wired for speed and efficiency. They are disconnected from your spirit, which is literally dying to slow down and reconnect with the rest of you and some peaceful, solitary moments with nature. Taking time to appreciate nature will help you do that. No matter how grand or seemingly sparse the natural beauty of your environment, it exists all around you. It is waiting for you to stop for a moment and simply notice it. What are some of the places near you that you have perhaps taken for granted and how close are they to you?

Perhaps you can plan a day trip or even a weekend getaway soon so that you can enjoy your "natural resources." Just as importantly, begin to notice the beauty in everyday nature—birds chirping, the gentle brush of wind against the leaves, or the rising and setting of the sun. Take a few minutes this week to go outside and bask in the beauty of life. Take a walk or stand outside and absorb the sights and sounds. It is a habit worth forming. In the midst of a hurried world, this practice can help your mind and body slow down long enough to experience the peace and serenity that makes your spirit sing!

# Journey To Success And Prosperity

## *The Color of Light*

### By Sandra M. Yee

Raised in an immigrant Chinese family, I'd been taught to save for the ever-foreboding rainy day—and it didn't rain much in southern Arizona.

We raised chickens and grew vegetables in our backyard. We kept defunct refrigerators and furniture on the back porch for storage, as we saved everything that "wasteful Americans" threw away—paper bags, plastic bags, foil, rubber bands, twist-ties, glass jars, margarine tubs. Our underwear and towels were stiff from being dried in the sun. My siblings and I were glad to inherit the neighbors' hand-me-downs so we didn't have to wear one another's anymore. We scrimped on toilet paper and skimped on flushes. Every meal was made at home.

An immigrant success story, my family sent five of us to college, but the need to pinch and scrimp and brace oneself against war and famine followed me into adulthood. I cut coupons, bought day-old produce, waited for clearance sales, and shopped at thrift stores.

When I splurged, I prayed my mother couldn't see me throwing money away on fine dining and multiple pairs of strappy, high-heeled sandals.

Shortly before the terrorist act of September 11, 2001, my soul mate and I bought our first home in Atlanta, Georgia. I was horrified already that my fun money had disappeared into our home's down payment and new appliances. I became near hysterical when our remaining savings took a dive in the next few months. I wasn't afraid of losing my life to a terrorist act; I was terrified of losing my retirement fund.

So began my journey to abundance. My mate could no longer find work in the technology industry, and my alternative-healing services did not bring enough income to support both of us in our new home. As my nagging and begging my mate to "take anything!" in the fallen IT industry failed, I trudged back into the corporate world myself.

Working as an administrative assistant for the first time in five years, I again pinched and scrimped and braced myself against war and famine. No more restaurant dining, salon visits, or mall shopping. I longed to repaint the mauve walls left behind by our home's previous owners. Every room in the house, including the garage and basement, had been coated in this dusty rose color, but my skimpy paycheck made decoration low on our list of priorities. Nonetheless,

I lusted for the perfect shade of yellow to lift me from my dark spirits. For two and a half years, I prowled paint sales and left with only dozens more paint chips.

I was juggling my corporate job and my natural-healing business at the same time, and as my reputation in natural medicine grew, I wrestled with the knowledge that I couldn't encourage people to use natural products on the body and in the home and then use cheap, toxic paint on my walls. And I couldn't counsel others on attracting prosperity into their lives when I was terrified of spending money on the wrong paint color.

With much opening and closing of the wallet, I finally decided to stop comparing prices and pay extra for earth-friendly, low-odor, low-toxin paint. In a few hours my soul mate and I erased the drab pink from the living room and welcomed "sunburst" into our home. Our walls pulsed with cheerful brightness. "I feel like I'm at the beach!" my mate cried out. My own heart filled with light.

All my life I had felt smug in living below my means. There was pride in denying myself luxuries and making do, and in the glow of that light-filled room, I saw the truth of my perverse vanity: I feared wealth. Anyone who had money and spent it on herself surely must be guilty and immoral, a shyster. I, who was humble and poor, or at least pretending to be, surely must be the good guy.

*Journey to Success and Prosperity*

Distancing myself from abundance, I distanced myself from authority. I was fearful of being too powerful, as in a leader or teacher. There'd be so much responsibility, so much freedom, so little excuse for not trying, and so little excuse for not being happy!

How naked I would feel without my chains.

Every day now I draw the shades wide open on our bright, sunny room. As the months pass, I increasingly recognize and release the weaknesses that keep me from living fully in my power. I was arrogant about what I could accomplish with so little—time, money, materials, whatever.

Now I imagine what the Divine can do through me, giving thanks for the resources that magically appear at the right time and place, and often from where I never expected it.

Our Creator longs to give us all we need to be powerful leaders, teachers, healers, mothers, and miracle workers. It is we who deny ourselves the right to be rich, and richly blessed. Raised in less affluent families and in a profit-driven culture, many of us go through life thinking that there is not enough, and especially not for someone as insignificant as me. In judging and being jealous of others for taking our piece of the pie, we fail to see that there is no pie.

Instead, there is infinite supply and it increases with the size of our hearts.

*When we trust in a kind and generous Universe, we expand our capacity for miracles.*

I trust in a kind and generous Universe, and trust that I have all that I need to be rich and richly blessed. My heart is open to receiving . . .

# *Freedom and Feasts*

## By Maria Denise Dowd

My daughters make my heart turn somersaults. Both are making movements into a freedom mind-set. And I'm euphoric. Each day, as I taste the kind of freedom that allows space to pursue my genius, my divine vocation, I long for my daughters to taste it, too. Each day I'm able to experiment with a new spice, herb, or entirely new recipe. How many of us are preparing our children to sit at the table with prosperity?

It starts in the test kitchens of the village—our family units, the community of elders and life outside the boundaries of our homesteads.

Recently, I watched an alarming special report about our children's increasingly poor school performance, even among the offspring of middle-class, college-educated parents. The reasons were plentiful, ranging from too much television, lack of parental involvement in school, a subconscious embracing and expectancy of low achievement, the stressors that come with working hard and long to attain and maintain basic standards of living, single parenting, lower incomes, parents blaming "the system," and hip-hop mind-sets that "poo poo" education for the "bling bling" of instant gratification.

There's a new call to the village to heighten its awareness and take extraordinary steps to reverse the bend of these trends. How might we begin to instill better practices and prepare our children to be free?

## At Home

Are we having dinner-table talks, or are we parking ourselves and our children in front of the television? And are our discussions centered on things that are important to our children? As their caretakers and life supporters, are we providing ample cups full of expressions centered on high achievement, wealth, making wise life choices, the perils of debt, home ownership, healthy eating, wholesome living, and how these things translate to family and community wellness and abundance? Do you feel qualified to discuss such things? Hmmm, what you discuss with your children could manifest for you.

A family "dream board" or collage is a powerful representation of values, hopes, and desires. Create it as a family unit, as well as individual ones, and display them in a special place with a special name, such as the Johnson's Family Abundance Gallery. Imagine the sense of pride and commitment to achieve greatness that could evolve from something as simple as an art project.

Fathers, get and stay involved with your children. Mothers, allow fathers and children that space. Adults, keep it wholesome, healthy, and drama-free. Children need to see and hear only what's right and good, not what's wrong and bad.

## At School

As parents, we have a responsibility to our children to help them succeed. Don't miss the open houses, parent/teacher conferences, and homework. Know the course work, schedules, and expectations, and have zero tolerance for procrastination, bad study habits, and bad attitudes. But, if you get the latter, investigate the source of the attitude. You never know what you might uncover.

Sacrifice *something* if your child needs a tutor, extra guidance, or counseling. Find ways to afford those things that enhance and attract wholesome experiences, but not those things that are nonsensical and distractions. Become their teacher's best friend, and stay connected with them to ensure that expectations and standards are being met, and hopefully exceeded. And, heighten your expectation and performance *as a parent*. Then, send a resounding message to both the teacher and your student that you plan to be a highly involved, no-nonsense parent.

Seek a computer and Internet access, well before the larger-screen television. And monitor your children's use like a prison guard. My daughter regularly used it to do research and taught herself to create some fabulous Power Point presentations for school projects. These skills are highly transferable to her prosperity plan.

If your child shows even a glimmer of brightness, *demand* that your children be placed in advanced classes. Bright children long to be challenged, although they may not admit it. Furthermore, the system can railroad our children into mediocre classes if we don't raise hell about it.

## Outside the Boundaries

The public library is free, and there are hundreds of resources and thousands of people who possess the wisdom, passion, and integrity to provide us with nourishing, balanced recipes for success and prosperity. Churches and schools can provide smorgasbords of support, but it takes the congregation of families—both by blood and by association—to ask for, and then to support, the support. Our ignorance, complacency, and inertia cost our families hundreds of thousands of dollars and our communities, billions.

The principles of prosperity are so basic; the same list appears over and over and over again in just about every wealth-related "how-to" book in circulation: value it, manage it, save it, invest it, make it, shield it, and share it. Some of us have this list committed to heart, and some are seeing it for the first time; most of us know some of its parts, but not the sum total. However, how many of us are teaching our children these principles? And how does that number compare with the numbers of us who are buying $150 sneakers for our children, yet not even giving the rundown on how many hours of work it took to purchase them? Better yet, how many of us are putting our sons and daughters to work to earn the money to buy their own $150 sneakers or weaves; or at the very least, making that purchase an award for maintaining an A-minus or B-plus average in the substantive classes (P.E. was not included in my calculations)?

Instead of going to the mindless movies, try an Artist Day, where each of you has ten or twenty dollars—the same amount you'd spend at the movies—and you travel to thrift stores, parks, and garage sales looking for treasures that signify your dreams. Then pick up treasure boxes at the dollar or thrift shop in which to place those treasures. Encourage your family members also to keep in their treasure boxes photos and letters to self and one another that speak to expectations, dreams, and desires. These letters may be in the form of affirmations, prose, or poetry.

*Journey to Success and Prosperity*

Get your child involved in life-enriching activities outside of the four walls of school, and possibly outside of *your* realm of experience... music, nontraditional sports (soccer, swimming, ice skating), arts, crafts, writing camps, Girl or Boy Scouts, outdoor camping. My youngest daughter played lacrosse, although to this day I don't understand the game. But she was the captain of her team, another transferable talent. My eldest daughter participated in a culturally diverse leadership camp one year and came back ecstatic about the weekend and quick to teach me a thing or two about people skills. Nope, I never claimed to be June Cleaver, but I was a conscientious mother and took her newfound wisdom to heart.

In between, there was the flute and oboe, the Science Institute, softball, charm school (that's a whole 'nother story!), and Girl Scout camp, where they slept under the stars, and fed, rode, and cleaned horses... and cursed me for the entire week. Years later, they still curse me for not disclosing the fullness of that experience, but vow to send *their* daughters to camp, to sleep under the stars and clean up after horses. Yes, they agree that with each shovel, a millisecond of character and humility was gained.

I saw another television special that interviewed children, who may have been around the age of seven, from various backgrounds. Too many of *our* children didn't even know the meaning of the word *vacation*. Yes, vacationing takes money, but let's wager on how many parents have spent weekends in Las Vegas or Atlantic City, but have never taken their children on a weekend camping trip. Fresh air, greenery, running water, and other natural things do wonders for the spirit. Slot machines do wonderful only for the chop-licking shareholders with really big bank accounts, houses, and lifestyles.

While we often drive home the notion that "money doesn't grow on trees," do you know—and teach your children—how money *can* grow? We need to encourage our children to ponder these concepts, and come up with ideas on how to make their own money. We'd be surprised at what our children will conjure up when invited to freely think outside the realms of possibilities. God gifts us with our calling, well before our conception, and most children start to display their talents, skills, and propensities very early. We owe it to them to acknowledge and encourage their exposure and development in these areas. My son-in-law was exposed to jazz as a young child, simply because his grandfather took him to see performances. Through this exposure and the support of his mother and family, today he's an accomplished trombonist, travels the world, and is currently producing his first CD. And he's been on this planet for only twenty-five years.

For nearly twenty years, he played on a borrowed trombone. I'd call his mother resourceful. As a single mother, she had to be. What about the village elder who loaned the instrument to Ryan for two decades? He's one of Ryan's earth angels, one of his many uncles—not related necessarily by blood, but certainly cosmically. Months after Ryan finally purchased his very first gently worn trombone, he was robbed at gunpoint. My daughter and he wrote letters to their circle of family and friends. The money was pooled and he got a replacement. Without his trombone, he couldn't make a living. Without a plasma-screen television or the latest and greatest video game... well, life goes on, and actually with greater quality. Our charge is to consider redirecting our resources into things that will enable our children to cast great nets, and to catch more fish for the feast.

## The Village

The elders in the village set the tone for values and ethics. The elders show up and support, consistently and wisely. They provide guidance, discipline, and enrichment.

Yes, not everyone comes to the table with the same dish. Some may bring steamed rice, while someone may bring swordfish; someone else may bring beans and another, steamed asparagus. What's most important is that we give our children ample and diverse tastes of life, and it starts at home, with us, their parents.

*You are the bows from which your children as living arrows are sent forth. The archer sees the mark upon the path of the infinite, and He bends you with His might that His arrows may go swift and far.*

                              Kahlil Gibran, *The Prophet*

The village needs me, and I need it to grow and flourish. Here are seven things I will do within the next thirty days that will support a child's divine calling . . .

# *Twenty-one*

## By Doreene Hamilton

**Tools Needed:** your creative mind, paper, writing utensil
**Time Needed:** fifteen minutes a day for twenty-one days
**Results:** clarity, obtaining your desire

You can change a pattern on the cellular level of your body in twenty-one days. You can also plant a desire on a cellular level in twenty-one days. What does this mean? It means you can stop smoking in twenty-one days. You can find a home or a job in twenty-one days. Does it sound too good to be true? Well, it's not. However, it does require work and dedication.

The hardest part of this process is getting clear about what you want. Very often you say you want something, for instance, a house. But do you know what kind of house you want? How many bedrooms or bathrooms do you want? Where is the house located? What are your neighbors like? Whether you realize it or not, you can create the type of home you want and the environment you want to live in. You can create a job, a car, or a new way of thinking in twenty-one days or less. What many people don't understand is that you are not given an idea without the means to achieve it. The house you create in your mind is out there. The job you want is out there.

It takes clarity, openness, and discipline to obtain anything you want. This process requires that you become an artist. You are designing the lifestyle you want. The power is in your pen. Each step of this exercise is categorized, and there is no limit to listing what you want. And because you are in control, you can change anything on your list at any time.

When you are ready, get comfortable. Prepare the beverage of your choice. Get a big notepad out and a pen or pencil. Your first statement at the top of your page defines what you want.

"I am now living in a house with the following characteristics."

"I am now working at a company with the following characteristics."

"I am now living a life with the following qualities."

If you are seeking a home or an apartment, start describing your home. Define the precise number of bedrooms and bathrooms you want, and how much closet space you need, or office space, if you need that. What kind of kitchen do you want? How big are the rooms? Do you need a backyard or a garage? Be clear. Walk around your home or someone else's home to get a feel for what you want or don't want.

If you are asking for a job don't feel you have to give the job a title. It's more important to describe the position. What will you do on a daily basis? What type of people will you work with? What is the salary range that you will be paid? I say range so you don't limit yourself, or eliminate yourself from the job. In describing your position, give yourself room to grow. How important is the distance between your job and your home? Is it important that they have a day-care facility nearby? Think about what's important to you and write it down.

Make a new consciousness your reality. Realize that you are a magnificent child of God. In knowing this, you know that all of your needs are met. Know that you are in divine health. Speak of your life in the way you desire it to be. Speak of your interactions with friends, family, and love relationships; your work and service projects; your finances, as well as your hopes, dreams, and desires. Speak of it all as if it is happening now and nothing can stop you. I assure you that this can bring profound changes in your life.

Once you've completed your list, review it for clarity. Does what you're asking for make sense? If you want a car that is less than four years old, you may be able to get it for a thousand dollars, but you should be willing to pay at least five. On the other hand, don't write that you are willing to pay two thousand dollars a month in rent if you know your comfort zone is eight hundred. Some things you shouldn't compromise on and only you know what they are. Remember, you are trying to manifest what you want, not what anyone else wants for you. Your request is private. It's not for your friends and family members to scrutinize. If you and your spouse are seeking a home or a car, you can work on the entire process together, but also know that you can work on it solo and still achieve the results you desire.

Your request doesn't have to be written as a list. You can write it in paragraph form or as a story. There is no set way to complete it. It's a matter of what works for you. When you have finished your list, give thanks to God, the Universe, or your chosen belief system.

Each day read your list three times. Read it first thing in the morning when your mind is clear. Read and visualize it. See yourself in that car, at that job, or in your home. Then release it. Do this process again midday and again before you go to bed at night. Doing it at bedtime carries the thought from your list into your subconscious mind as you rest. As you sleep, your subconscious gets clearer on exactly what you want.

Within two weeks you will begin to see manifestations of what you want. You'll meet people who are doing the job you described, or you'll see homes that are similar to the one you want.

It's important not to attempt to use this technique in a negative fashion. You can't use it to get a mate that is not interested in you. You can't use it to get someone to sell his or her car to you for a lower price. Nor can you use it to get someone else's job or house. Your good is out there; don't try to take someone else's. Claim yours.

This technique works. I always tell people to be careful of what you ask for, because you'll get it. Don't ask for a new place if you're not ready to move. As you work your request, start preparing for it. Obtain clothes for your job interview, or get your finances in order for your new home. Are you ready for your good? Are you ready to take the steps: to write out the statement of your desire; to recite it three times a day; to prepare yourself for the manifestations; to repeat the process for twenty-one days; then trust that the Universe will take care of the rest?

# *Power of the Pixie*

## By Rhonda Kuykendall-Jabari

My friends are fairies of the rarest sort. We met under precocious circumstances at various inner-city schools in Los Angeles. We were about nine years old. Even then, we possessed a certain quality that would later reveal itself as the Power of the Pixie.

According to the legend I made up, Ephemina is the land where women are conceived, long before birth. It is there that each woman's Pixie is perfected. According to Ephemina legend, Wisdoria is the Goddess of wise womanness. She orchestrates the spiritual development of every woman's "she-power." At a Conception Ceremony, a pouch containing precious dust finds the female essence for whom it was created. With Pixie dust and pouch embedded in her soul, each female essence becomes a girl-child. It is every girl's responsibility to care for and maintain her Pixie dust and pouch for all of her days on earth.

The Power of the Pixie is a choice to care purposefully for that deepest part of ourselves that connects us to our highest power. To properly maintain Pixie dust, we must love ourselves unconditionally, forgive our past transgressions, live balanced lives, and answer to our higher calling from the Universe. These things greatly enhance the life force of our Pixie dust, keeping it vibrant and ensuring that it resonates with our souls in perfect harmony. We are attractive to everyone and maintain a healthy sense of self-worth. Guided by the Divinity within, women with powerful Pixie dust develop fulfilling and loving relationships and relate well to other women. Friendships are nurturing and free from drama, and confidences are kept. Children thrive safely and wholly in our presence. Our beauty is timeless, exuding a healthful glow whether we are bare-faced in paint-stained coveralls, or finely made up in an evening gown. Abundance and joy are with us always.

Neglected Pixie dust is faded, dull, and clumped. It would be great if we could keep it hidden, but static leaks from the worn bags attract negative energy everywhere we go. We work too hard, play too much, eat the wrong foods, and live unhappy lives. We fail to love or care for ourselves and have no friends for support in times of need. We plod through a string of toxic relationships, ending in self-deprecation and sorrow. Grayed and moldy, our Pixie dust attracts women-friends who are combative, deceitful, and hurtful. Children fail to develop into healthy adults in our care, and we become caged victims of our own poor decision-making. Scarcity is ever-present, causing feelings of desperation and despair.

The beauty of Pixie dust is that it is completely forgiving. Total restoration and renewal are possible at any time, regardless of the duration and severity of neglect. We can reclaim a life of happiness and fulfillment by taking steps to heal and rejuvenate our Pixie dust. This is the reward of self-love and enhanced self-care. We can claim it at any time. No apologies. No excuses. All that is needed is continuous care of our own heart and spirit, and trust that our commitment to treating ourselves well will yield desired results of restored inner and outer beauty, balance, and peace of mind.

My fairy friends are constant gauges of how well I'm caring for my Pixie dust. They alert me to the dangers of self-neglect and remind me to love and forgive myself unconditionally. Needless to say, these friendships were developed when my dust was most vibrant and fresh. When I find myself slipping, I take swift and deliberate steps to salvage my pouch and dust before clumping begins.

When you feel ill effects of contaminated and caked Pixie dust, stop. Take time to focus inward, ask for what you need, and give thanks through prayer or meditation. Cleanse and detoxify your body temple with herbs and plenty of fresh drinking water. Go on a talk fast for twenty-four hours to allow time for reflection and receive Divine guidance. Speak the truth. Trust that your words will be received in the spirit in which they are intended. Your Pixie is at risk and now is no time for self-sacrifice. There is no nobility in losing the Power of your Pixie. Be selfish; close your store, the one where others pull from your shelves to restock their supply of love, patience, energy, and time. Invest wisely in the maintenance and preservation of your Pixie dust and pouch. The rewards are fulfillment, optimal wellness, vibrant energy, peace of mind, and a connectedness with your higher power that readily transfers your deepest desires into reality from a simple thought. It is work that only you can do.

My sacred pouch is filled will all sorts of treasures, gifts, hopes, dreams, and desires. As I pull open the ties and peer inside, all of these wonder-filled things spill onto my lap. I'm thrilled to be in possession of all of these amazing things. Describe them. . . .

# *Life Savers Come in Red and Green*

## By Maria Denise Dowd

A funny thing happened on the way home from the bank. I *finally* learned to say "no." And it tasted like my favorite Life Savers.

I remember the very moment I started peeling away the tightly stamped foil wrappings. It happened at a conference about three years ago when Mary, an adviser on women's financial health, asked the darnedest question:

"You know who the biggest pimps in our lives are?" It was posed as a question, yet delivered like a politician's proclamation.

"No," we softly replied. I'm certain that most of the divorced mothers were inaudible.

"Our children."

It was the funniest thing I'd heard and affirmed all day.

Several months later I was channel-surfing and happened upon a show featuring a popular financial adviser who was on the phone, edgily listening to a single mother sing the cash flow/cash crunch/cash hemorrhage blues, droning on about her struggles to pay her bills that included her grown daughter's car note. The show host was obviously dying to jump in and stop the woman in her tracks.

The woman, now kinda sorta stuttering on the other side of the wires, didn't initially own up to the car payment obligation right away. But leave it up to the host—who's a true psychic in her own right—to pry it out of woman. Then, she proceeded to tell the poor divorcée off.

"So, why are you carrying an adult's car note and you're struggling to meet your basic day-to-day needs, not to mention neglecting to put away for your retirement?" True to her "keep it real" fashion, she asked it in a tone that suggested, "Woman, are you nuts?"

As I listened, her words reverberated against the walls of my frame of mind. Those crevices beneath my ears and along my jawline began to anticipate the sour-sweetness of the hard candy. Hmm, how would "no" encircle my lips and roll off my tongue like a syrupy gust of breath? Readying to stick my thumbnail between that rock and that hard place, I pondered my breakthrough. After all, I'd been feeding on others' experiences and notions of kindheartedness and obligation, blended with bullying and that chewy thing called "mommy guilt." What was it going to taste like to no longer haphazardly hand control of my Life Savers roll over to my two darling princesses?

More recently, as I was still sucking on my candy, the phone rang. I answered it. On the other end was one of my princesses asking for a short-term loan. I'd tallied this as her third call and my second "no." Yummy.

This time she suggested that I dip into my waaaay-less-than-adequate, post-9/11 retirement fund to loan her a thousand dollars... just for a couple of days, she footnoted.

I reared back, jostled that dissolving Life Saver into my cheek for safekeeping, and to keep from choking, and I asked:

"Woman, are you nuts?"

Then hung up the phone, popped a green one into my mouth, and went about my merry way.

Later that month during a visit to my princess's home, true to mommy form, I asked her if she'd worked out her money situation. Her reply touched my spirit.

"I figured out that I was forcing something to happen and it wasn't my Divine Time."

I nestled back in the seat of her newly purchased snow-white Mustang convertible (that *she's* paying for), rolling my green Life Saver into the other cheek, and said to her, "Good for you."

Give yourself permission to just say no to the things that are zapping your resources and taking you down an uncomfortable path. Describe what those things are and write down one action step that you'll take today to relieve your ache, build your cash flow, and bring yourself one step closer to financial freedom. . . .

# *A Higher Plateau*

## By Gequeta Valentine

Beautiful, bountiful success. That was all I'd ever wanted to achieve, and for a long time I believed it was all I'd ever need to fully appreciate life and all it had to offer. Never once during my relentless pursuit to reach my delicately designed apex did I ever stop to think about what *I* could offer *it*. Without looking back I thrust myself into the mesmerizing mirage of éclat. Blinded, I gripped life by its bullhorns and rode the turbulent broadside of its rugged terrain toward my preordained destiny. And it was there at the threshold of my achievement, the culmination of my hopes and dreams, that I felt the enormity of what I'd requested from the Universe. With both feet securely planted on the last tread of my journey and my shaking hands at my side, I breathed a victorious sigh of relief. I looked up toward heaven and silently basked in its generosity. I had finally achieved what I had so long strived for. Although my hands and clothes were soiled with the muck and mire of life's many obstacles, my mind was pristine, free and clear from all that had plagued me throughout my voyage. Self-doubt, mishaps, opposition, and disappointments were many, but were now vanquished. Sacrifice and sheer determination had prevailed. Elated with the thought of my imminent victory, I raised my clutched fist in triumph and looked down to fully assess the landscape over which I had desperately traveled. What my eyes gazed upon would forever change me as I stared into the pleading eyes of a woman whom I vaguely recognized, a woman whose features strangely resembled my own. Arm extended, she reached her hand forward to grasp mine, periodically looking behind her at a dense fog where her other hand had disappeared. Stunned, I watched her frustration for what seemed like an eternity. She continued to stretch forth her hand, feverishly waving it to emphasize her urgency, until finally, she bowed her head in defeat and rested her hand on my ankle. An indescribable force surged through my body at the touch. Startled, I knocked her hand away and quickly reached upward toward my expectancy. I turned around to look once again at the peak that awaited me, ready to be mounted. But as I stared at its vastness, images of my people, diligently plowing and marching through decades of despair, danced through my mind in full animation. For them, no ladders had been erected or trails blazed, yet they still reached back and pulled others along the way, including myself, a product of a thankless generation that has yet to realize the true essence of strength, tenacity, and triumph. How arrogant of me to believe that what I had managed to accomplish had been solely of my own doing, as if I hadn't received an extended hand, a word of encouragement, a shoulder of support, a bit of shared knowledge, an ancestral legacy, or a simple admiration for a steadfast role model. Where would I be had that not been provided to me? Suddenly reaching my destination seemed so unimportant, self-centered even. The time had come for me to be accountable, for me to take my turn at giving back to life what it had given to me. So with all the strength I could muster, I reached out my hand toward the young woman and beckoned her to take hold of it. Leaving the sacred spot of my mind's eye, I sprang forward, grabbed her free hand with my two, and pulled her toward me, closing the distance between us. As I continued to pull, her body began to come into full view. As she emerged, another hand and body came into view, and then another, and another, and another until each hand intertwined forming a human chain across the deep horizon for the entire world to see and hopefully one day emulate our commitment to elevate and empower, not just ourselves, but each other.

# Seeds for Abundance

## By Shu Oce Ani

The *abundance* of the Universe must begin with the *abundance* of the individual. When I cocreate with others in fulfilling their goals and dreams, I also create for my-*Self*. We are all *ONE*, we are all waves in the same ocean and one person's consciousness of *abundance* and well-being releases more *abundance* and *prosperity* into the Universe. So I begin with myself:

I am the Spirit of Infinite Plenty individualized
I am boundless abundance in radiant expression
I am abundance and I demonstrate it in everything I do
I am the energy of money made visible
I am the expression of boundless wealth in the universe
I am the wealth of the universe individualized
I am the pure energy of abundance that expresses itself for the joy of it
I am a mighty money magnet and oceans of money engulf me
I am wonderfully rich in consciousness

I am the continuous flow of money that is used with love and wisdom
I am unlimited prosperity
I am alert to my opportunities and I use them well
I am an unlimited being, I can create anything I want
I am a magnificent and powerful being
I am increasingly magnetic to money, prosperity, and abundance

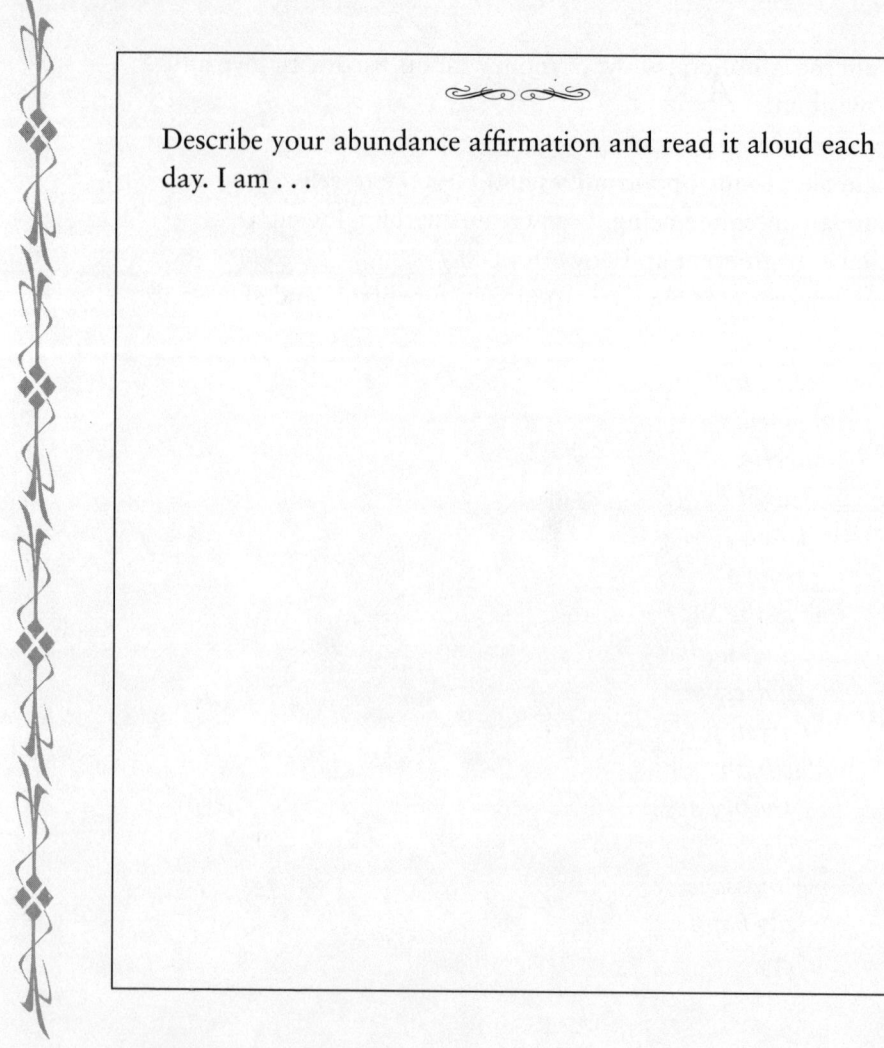

Describe your abundance affirmation and read it aloud each day. I am . . .

# A Woman's Treasures

## By Ann Clay

*Falling in love.*
*Chocolate anything!*
*Someone telling you that you're beautiful.*
*New lingerie.*
*A girls' night out.*
*A love letter.*
*A card from a dear friend.*
*No line at the Super Wal-Mart.*
*Cuddling up with a significant other on a rainy day.*
*Finding a dress you want on sale for half price . . .*
*Or better yet, for 75 percent off.*
*A bubble bath.*
*Finding twenty dollars in your coat pocket from last winter.*
*A massage.*
*Another massage.*
*Small daily happenings that makes life so spectacular.*
*A good cry.*

*A good movie and a good cry.*
*No panty lines.*
*Did I say chocolate . . . more chocolate!*
*Acknowledgment.*

# *Rivers of Abundance*

## By Rafiki Cai

Overflowing. Plenteous. Copious. Superfluous.

Imagine these four rivers continuously flowing through our lives...

Acting as forces that drive our plans and actions to complete fruition...

Serving sources that nourish our legacies one hundred years from now.

Imagine... How do we come to realize this vision?

We must first acutely understand and engage the abundance that *does* course through our lives already. And we must do so *right now*, not when we earn that second degree, or move into that exclusive development, or manage to make that right investment; but right now, today. Second, we must learn how to tap, direct, and harness these rivers, so that power is brought forth from their presence.

In step number one, it's important to underscore the difference between reality and perception, as well as between kinetic and potential states. Things are not necessarily as we see and experience them, or as we frame and process them, but rather as they are. What does this mean? Simply put: we can, in fact, be rich and in the midst of abundance, but endure a life of lack, destitution, and poverty.

On the surface such a claim doesn't seem to make sense. Our knee-jerk reaction is "Who on earth would be wealthy and allow themselves to suffer through the pains of indigence?" The answer may well be you and I.

The reality is that there exists a great deal of wealth in each of our lives. Yet, our perceptions often blind us to this actuality. The filters and cataracts that distort our vision can be many and with varied points of origin. Some of our distortions, in fact, were acquired from our most trusted sources: family, mates, colleagues, and religious advisers. In many cases, we've inherited or accepted their perceptions as our own, not always being fully aware of the dangers of such transfusions.

## Perception One in Life: Who We Are

Depending on our upbringing, we have been told that we are "sinful by nature," "shaped in iniquity," "not the same as a man (or other men)," "inferior," "human," and a sundry list of other things, each of which affects our "sight" and helps to shape our sense of reality. Even if we've been encouraged toward strong and clear vision, torrential comments and beliefs can affect us just enough to render our seeing faculties flawed.

Our sight influences our steps and movement, and determines whether we scuffle and stumble, or soar and stride through life. It guides whom we associate with, what we reach for, and what we expect from life.

In such a condition one can easily be quite intelligent, yet reality-blind, resulting in our ability to talk a superb game, while not truly seeing what we're mouthing. The truth of what we're doing eventually shows up in our state of being, our *flow*. With a simple two-column ledger, we can measure our flow intensity—or our Abundance Quotient, a.k.a. "AQ," as I like to call it. Within such a scenario the left-hand column reads "Potential" and the right-hand column, "Kinetic." Under Potential, we tally what we're capable of, what we have in hand, and what's right within our grasp. Under "Kinetic," we calculate what we're doing, what we're engaging and applying, and what we're sowing. The difference between the two columns equals our AQ—our experiential abundance—that which we live, experience, and enjoy right now.

What's the sum total of your two columns?

How do we move items from our Potential column over to our more powerful Kinetic column? How do we go about more effectively tapping the abundance that is within us, and all around us? A few answers to this question are: See. Organize. Execute.

*Journey to Success and Prosperity*

A key element to *seeing* more is actually imagining yourself successfully in the roles and positions where you need to be in order to realize full prosperity. Do what you must to create this "clearer sight." Role-play. Craft short stories, poems, news articles, press releases, songs, acceptance speeches, for instance. Try your hand at them all. Run your success throughout all of your senses, as though it were actually happening right before your eyes. When you do this, the amazing thing is that your mind will not know the difference between this immersion and what we call reality. It will react accordingly and beckon the forces of Creation to shape physically the things that it has "seen."

In the context of potential versus kinetic, or "actual," a good deal of our abundance slips away from us because we are not good stewards of the seeds and processes that would bring it forward. How many people have you met within the past year who could possibly have lent a supportive hand to your success? How many times have you taken the card or contact information of such people, and then not followed up appropriately and regularly? Do you even know where their information is right now?

A very important metaphysical insight to weigh is our need to be at the right point in the flow. Perhaps *you're* to be a helping hand to another person's forward movement. In turn, that helpful energy will come back around to you, even if not directly from that particular person. By being out of flow, we can block the turning of many a

*Journey to a Blissful Life*

waterwheel: your own, someone else's, and possibly a third or fourth party who was to be aided in the forward flow process. In light of this critical fact, pull yourself together and get with it. Planning and preparation is fine. Doing something is even better. Align yourself with people who are about "the do." Action is a kinetic energy, which draws to itself, leans toward magnification, and feeds quantum leaps. Bodies at rest are apt to remain there and consequently attract stagnation, arrested development, and dissipation.

To be more, you've got to do more. Period. No more words without actions to back them. Just do it. Intend to succeed. And if you don't, do it again and again and again. Each time around, tune in ever more intently for the missed turns and the clues of sabotage, from internal and external sources, but don't stop doing. Consider collaborations, especially around the areas in which you're not strong. There is enough for you to reap and share, more than enough. Get over the fears and the grudges from ten or twenty years ago and get busy. Your abundance may be stagnating while your temper or attitude is brewing.

If you earnestly do these things, your life won't be the same. In metaphysical fact it will be, but you will have peeled back layers of illusion that were hiding the abundance that was there all the time. When you begin to sense and see the appearance of more of the real you, celebrate and bathe your life in gratitude. This vibration can empower you to peel back even more layers, and more layers, to the point where you'll find yourself so far from where you started out that it'll be utterly amazing. When you get there, drop a brother a few lines; wherever I am, I'd like to toast your arrival and give thanks for yet another unblocking of the river that is Oneness and Endless Abundance.

Today I will take greater strides to move more of my potentials into my Kinetic column to advance toward a more abundant life. Here is a list of my potentials and an action step I will take to increase my abundance quotient . . .

# *Praise and Prosperity for the Priestesses*

## By Sandra M. Yee

When you meet a woman who is living her truth, who has helped see your own truth more clearly, drop to your knees and give thanks. Honor her as a light-bearer with love, with praise, and yes, with funding. Money is another form of love: the more given, the more received.

When we support women who are living their dreams—those magical women who devote their everyday lives to their spiritual gifts, whether it be in healing, teaching, business consulting, ministering, the creative arts, motherhood, or all of the above—we enable them to help so many others find their wings, including our own.

For more information on Maria Dowd's Journey to Empowerment seminars, speaking opportunities, or inspirational gifts, or to purchase a copy of *Journey to Empowerment*, this book's older sister (BET Books; ISBN 1-58314-494-3), contact Soul Journeys, Inc., P.O. Box 152107, San Diego, CA 92195-2107, 1-800-560-2298, maria@aawot.com, http://www.aawot.com.